GUERRILLA TIME

GUERRILLA TIME

TIME

More Time In Your Life,
More Life In Your Time

JAY CONRAD LEVINSON
& ANDREA FRAUSIN

NEW YORK

GUERRILLA TIME
More Time In Your Life, More Life In Your Time

© 2014 **JAY CONRAD LEVINSON & ANDREA FRAUSIN.**

Published in New York, New York, by Morgan James Publishing. Morgan James and The Entrepreneurial Publisher are trademarks of Morgan James, LLC.
www.MorganJamesPublishing.com

The Morgan James Speakers Group can bring authors to your live event. For more information or to book an event visit The Morgan James Speakers Group at www.TheMorganJamesSpeakersGroup.com.

FREE eBook edition for your existing eReader with purchase

_____
PRINT NAME ABOVE

For more information, instructions, restrictions, and to register your copy, go to **www.bitlit.ca/readers/register** or use your QR Reader to scan the barcode:

ISBN 978-1-61448-959-7 paperback
ISBN 978-1-61448-960-3 eBook
ISBN 978-1-61448-962-7 hardcover
Library of Congress Control Number:
2013949909

Cover Design by:
Rachel Lopez
www.r2cdesign.com

Interior Design by:
Bonnie Bushman
bonnie@caboodlegraphics.com

In an effort to support local communities, raise awareness and funds, Morgan James Publishing donates a percentage of all book sales for the life of each book to Habitat for Humanity Peninsula and Greater Williamsburg.

Get involved today, visit
www.MorganJamesBuilds.com

Habitat for Humanity
Peninsula and
Greater Williamsburg
Building Partner

DEDICATION

To Leonardo, to Nicolas John and to all young people
    everywhere
To Sylvia, the love of my life
To my parents Fulvio and Biancamaria
To John Grinder, no words can explain how grateful I am
    to you John, thank you
To Carmen Bostic St. Clair, thank you Carmen for
    insisting on intention
To Jay Conrad Levinson, the Guerrilla who insisted I put
    my knowledge into print
To all the people I met and interacted with: you gave me
    the experience on which this book is based.

Andrea Frausin

TABLE OF CONTENTS

INTRODUCTION

by Jay Levinson

"**I have read many** books about time and time management but this book goes far beyond those. I suggest that you read it, use it, practice and surprise yourself with the enhancements in the quality of your life. Your productivity, performance, and satisfaction will increase well beyond your expectations. Time is life; time is the most strategic variable in Guerrilla Marketing.

Andrea, you've done it! I am proud you are a Guerrilla Marketing Master Trainer.

Jay Conrad Levinson

FOREWORD

by Dr. John Grinder

Our home planet circles our sun once every 365 days (more or less) and we experience cycles of light and darkness called day and night: periods correlated with the changing tilt of the axis of the earth relative to our sun. These periods shift significantly in duration over the course of our travel around the sun. And yes, it is true that we have circadian rhythms set up and regulated by special receptors in our physiology and neurology natural structure entrained by millions of years of evolution and attuned to portions of the natural environment such as the light conditions.

These natural chronometers are not the issue they are loose enough and their edges are soft enough to allow significant degrees of freedom within which we can both exercise choice and still coordinate our movements and activities with the world around us.

Take a look around next time you are in a gathering of people. Some are slaves of time, some are not.

How can you tell the difference? Well there are some obvious markers: some, for example, wear the marker of time slaves—that ubiquitous wrist watch. This is slightly unfair as I do know women and some men who wear wristwatches for fashion. Others actually have responsibilities that require that they perform certain actions at precise times (experimenters, airline pilots, investigators…). However the majority seem to wear this special slave of time marker voluntarily.

Worst than wearing a time piece, you can spot these slaves of time by their frequent, furtive glances at their watch, smart phone or some prominent public clock. Their muscle tonus is excessive and the breathing cycle tends to be high in their chest, rapid and shallow. They never actually arrive at the location that they are physically present at. They typically lean into the future: while physically present at location X, their attention is anywhere but on the people and events at location X.

One of the most telling indicators shows up if you ask them a simple question

Are you hungry?

Their response to that question is most instructive. What do they do when asked this question… they look at their watch. Long gone are the days when body sensations serve as the reference point that they used to know how to respond to this question. They are eating on the clock.

Listen to the form that these slaves of time use to ask their questions,

Say, do you have time _____? (for a conversation, for a cup of coffee, for a walk down by the water, to drop by Jimmy's to see how he is doing…)

How many of your daily activities are on the clock?

Think back to your early days when you had a life and the freedom to choose on the spot what you wanted to do. Now, how the hell did you get from there to slave of time status? When did you turn over that set of choices to this strange human invention called TIME? By what series of decisions did you abdicate perhaps the single most important responsibility for your life—what you will do WHEN!

So, what Guerrilla Time is, is a step towards recovering those choices, of living by what you wish when you wish to do it as opposed to a mindless schedule driven not by where you find yourself, with whom you find yourselves or, indeed, what you wish to do with the rich set of opportunities you find yourself in the midst of. Seize this opportunity and make your life the one that you want to live!

John Grinder
Bonny Doon, California
September 2012

NOTE FROM THE TRANSLATOR

Thomas J. Keeler and SavvyTranslation

As a translator most of the time you have a text containing ideas, and the ideas can be familiar or unfamiliar, as can be the words themselves. Rarely do you know the author personally, consult with him on his *intention*, get to know his mind and really start to feel when your text is almost exactly as he would have put it if he were native to your land.

With Guerrilla Time I had that opportunity, allowing me to know the text from inside the mind of the author, rather than solely from the PDF that was delivered to me at the beginning of this adventure. Therefore when you read, dear reader, forget that it was my hand that struck the keyboard with letters of English ilk, since the author himself has said of this text *"I'm amazed... I hear my own voice as I read! As if I'd written the English myself."*

In other words, rather than see this book as a translation of Andrea by Thomas, see it as Andrea borrowing words from Thomas, borrowing the frame for his ideas, borrowing the code for English-speaking minds. Like this it's clear that one man alone wrote this book... and his name is Andrea Frausin.

Thomas J. Keeler
www.savvytranslation.com

CHAPTER 1

THE NEED FOR GUERRILLA TIME

"Heavier-than-air flying machines are impossible"
(Lord Kelvin, physicist and former President of the Royal Society, 1895)

"Airplanes will never travel as fast as trains"
(William Henry Pickering, Astronomer, Harvard college, 1908)

"Guitar groups are on the way out, Mr. Epstein"
(Dick Rowe, Decca records, on The Beatles' audition at Decca Records on January 1st, 1962)

"Time is money" (many authors, -2013)

All Guerrillas know time is more, much more, than money. Time is life and the quality of our time is the quality of our lives.

What value do you give to your time?

If you're one of those "I haven't got time" people, or if you're always saying to yourself "If I only had more time," or if you think that the quality of your life could be improved, then you're in luck: this book is for you!

It's All About YOU!

This book is not about time management. This book is about you.

It's about your needs, your emotions and your dreams. It's about your virtues and your faults. It's about your great potential and your many talents, be these hidden away or clear for all to see. You and only you!

This book speaks to every human being.

It's written for human beings, for people who dramatically want to improve themselves and the quality of their lives. People made of flesh and blood, people like you and me... real Guerrillas of Time.

Who are these people?

How do we spot these Guerrillas of Time? Well...

- you may see them fully enjoying life in the most unexpected ways (they understand themselves to be the best judges of their actions and don't hang on the expectations of others)
- sometimes they're happy, sometimes reflective, sometimes brilliant... they have a myriad of times and are a kaleidoscope of states.... each chosen deliberately by these particular people
- they know when to stop and when to carry on; they understand their own needs—their superficial needs and, above all, their deep needs; they know what must be done in order to feel better now, or if not now then at least not long from now
- they know what they want and they really want it
- sometimes they change their minds, which can be the wisest move
- they know how to be humble and resolute
- they are fully involved in listening whenever they decide to be so. They know how to be in the here and now, eyes open, ears pricked, senses tuned; living the "here and now" is truly a choice available to them
- they know how to withhold judgment
- they're curious
- they know how to plan without becoming a victim of planning
- they're able not to plan, yet do not wander, unless by choosing wandering
- they know how to enjoy a beautiful sunset and how to enjoy the rain, they know the pleasure of a single step on a long journey, whether first or last or one of the steps in between

- they know that life can be a work of art… a masterpiece of theatre in which they play the lead

- _____

- _____

- _____

- _____

- _____

- _____

- _____

In the spaces above I'd like you to write down what you really want and… start to write your masterpiece!

Thousands and Thousands of Books on Time Management Which Forget About…

Of the thousands of books on the topic "time management" many of them will have forgotten about an essential element….

That's right, you!

These books are little more than collections of "technical advice", which becomes extremely hard to implement if the human element is left out, as, alas, often happens.

When it does happen, in a sense sweeping the issue under the carpet, time management may still bring some progress.

But what progress exactly?

Perhaps a spare thirty minutes here and there? We can hope!

What kind of time will this be and what value will it have?

If it's not centered around you, if your needs as a human being, as a person, are not the keynotes in the symphony, then the quality of your life will not be as good as it might be.

What do I promise?

Miracles, magic solutions? Absolutely not!

What I promise is that, having read this book, you'll have all it takes to become a real Guerrilla of Time.

You'll learn all the essentials, all the elements, from the simplest to the most complex.

As you now know, you spot a Guerrilla by noticing that he or she acts where others simply acknowledge things or stare. If you truly want to augment the quality of your time, roll up your sleeves and practice, practice, practice what you find on these pages, making from the ingredients there listed the recipe for what you truly desire.

It won't be simple. You'll have to face a very important person, very important indeed. That person, of course, is you.

You, with your habits, with your faults, with your praiseworthy qualities. It'll be hard at times.

Some Indian tribes use a special technique for taming elephants.

From a young age, the elephant is tied to a pole by a strong rope. The little elephant tries and tries, unsuccessfully, to get away from the pole.

His determination is to no avail… The pole is too big and the rope too strong.

As time passes, attempts become fewer, until the day he knows exactly how far he can go. His world is bound by an invisible circle. This is his explorable world. Then, once he has grown up big and strong, we are confronted by the remarkably strange sight of a tiny pole holding a behemoth at bay. He, of course, doesn't see things this way. One more try and he'd burst through the wall of his invisible bubble… but instead he keeps on wandering, round and round his world.

When you come to explore unfamiliar or even entirely unknown lands, you won't be alone. The tools you will find in this book will be with you, as will your fellow adventurers on this journey.

Your satisfaction at, finally, fully feeling yourself, with an ocean of new choices and opportunities before you, with your quality of life ever on the rise, perhaps to the surprise of those around you, will serve as ample reward for having undertaken this adventurous journey.

But don't wait for these things to be before enjoying life. Enjoy the whole journey. Every single step you take, every word you read, every piece of advice you consider, every tool you put into action with disciplined practice. Too often, instead of rewarding ourselves and enjoying our time, we wait for goals beyond our reach to be met. Why bind ourselves this way? Why wait, wait and wait some more?

Don't be satisfied with the first fruits borne of your endeavors, yet fully enjoy these fruits as they come to you… continue to look around, carefully listening, fully feeling every experience—the possibilities are endless. And when you fully enjoy the single moments of your life and you notice the quality of your life increasing significantly, in that moment—and that moment only—will you be a Guerrilla of Time.

If you think I've forgotten anything important, please let me know: It's always, without exception, possible to improve.

CHAPTER 2

7+ DIFFERENCES BETWEEN TRADITIONAL TIME MANAGEMENT (TTM) AND GUERRILLA TIME (GT)

here are some major differences between traditional time management and Guerrilla Time. Understanding them will help cast light on the path to becoming a Guerrilla of Time.

1. TTM Is Mainly About Techniques vs. GT Is About You

Traditional time management essentially focuses on techniques. Guerrilla Time is about you: It's about your needs, your virtues, your faults. Too often time management advice is difficult to apply. Despite discipline in implementation, the advice tends to turn your habits upside down, to the point where you effectively refuse to make use of it. The worst outcome is that you feel like it's you that isn't working, that something's wrong with you—the advice is fine, it's just that you can't make it work.

You might feel inadequate and helpless, even worse than how you felt before you started applying the techniques. They tell you: "Now you have the necessary awareness. You know the tricks of time management"—traditional time management, by the way—"These techniques work very well. It's you that's not working!" And if the training session is paid for by your company, well, it's no wonder they say it's your fault.

You'll be happy to know you're not alone. There are many people like you, who barely apply a fraction of what they are taught in traditional time management. You're not what's not working here!

You work, you really do!!!

Cyborgs can make TTM work. They're able to apply its techniques. For humans, it's a different story altogether.

2. TTM Is Based on … vs. GT Is Based on the Evolution of Personal and Professional Development

Many traditional time management techniques, lacking in the wisdom that you will acquire from this book, work very well, when run on computers. You, like me, are a human being.

This is why Guerrilla Time is based on the most recent advances in personal and professional development and in the study of human psychology. Thanks to these solid foundations, Guerrilla Time is the best tool you'll have to make the best of your time.

It gives you the techniques to do this. More than 150 weapons to enormously increase the value of your time. The thing it cares about most, however, is what I call the human factor. You'll read about this throughout the book, finding reference to it over and over again. You'll be invited to practice it yourself. It's the thing that makes the difference. I'll never tire of mentioning it. You really mustn't forget about it. And, most importantly, you should make it part of your daily life.

As you combine techniques with the human factor, what you already know will take on a new light. Things that didn't work before will start to work.

When you discover the pleasure of being yourself, you'll be a Guerrilla of Time.

3. TTM Is Mainly Left Brain vs. GT Is
a Fine Balance Between Left and Right Brain

Traditional time management is generally very rational, being based on the logic of the so-called "dominant hemisphere". This is why many people fall into the trap of "feeling inadequate". From a purely deductive perspective of cause and effect, everything seems to work. And so we ask ourselves: Why, then, isn't it working for me? Am I irrational? Do I need to be fixed? Am I abnormal?

Guerrilla Time reveals to you the magician from a privileged viewpoint. You can see his tricks. You can understand that your intuition is right most of the time. You can understand why techniques by themselves don't work.

Guerrilla Time is based on harmony, the dynamic balance between left and right hemisphere, between voluntary and involuntary processes, between reason and intuition. You'll get the best out of this balance. Your talents will emerge. The things that I tell you will become your own, as will many other things that you'll discover by yourself as you follow this book's suggestions and take heed of its insights. Day after day the quality of your life experience will change, changes that won't be limited to your time management or to your productivity. Fulfillment, pleasure, self-effectiveness—you'll act differently, you'll feel different. And you'll notice how this development process just keeps on going!

4. TTM Is Difficult to Act upon vs. GT Is Easy to Understand and Requires Disciplined Actions

I don't want to delude you—it will be difficult! It takes energy, commitment and focus. In particular, three things (or one very important thing if we insist on being literal) must be carried out with great discipline:

practice
practice
practice

And you won't learn anything of worth from this book if not through three other things (again, literally one very important thing):

action

action

action

So why do these singular things come in threes? Well, simply put, it's a metaphor, and for good reason a common one. Twice is a metaphor for plurality. It suggests the occurrence is not unique, that it's more than pure chance. Thrice, however, is a metaphor for continuity. And with these requisites, continuity is key!

Guerrilla Time focuses on the human factor, on you. You'll discover how to take your deepest needs into account, how to sense signals from your body and how to pay attention to them. You will understand how to overcome your inner limits, your internal brakes, converting them into the accelerators of your success.

5. TTM Is "the Truth" vs. GT Is Your Learning Experience

You'll also learn about another tragic error made in traditional time management. What I tell you is NOT "the Truth", but rather a mixture of ideas, tools and suggestions which may turn out to be very useful. Yet most important of all is that you learn from your experience and that you truly make the things you read in this book your own. After practicing, you'll discover new things on your path of learning, you'll see what works for you and you'll tell us about your discoveries, those personal inventions which improve the quality of your life. Guerrilla Time is continuously expanding. It's a work in progress. Guerrilla Time is a learning community. Guerrilla Time is feedback. Whenever Guerrillas gather together... exceptional things can happen. Guerrillas working together form a knowledge base which is constantly updated and which has the power to improve the lives of many people.

While traditional time management says it represents the truth, Guerrilla Time is honest. Guerrilla Time is your learning experience. No one thing nor person can replace it. And it's the result that matters: your satisfaction, your pleasure, your living of your life in a way which is different and more rewarding for you. And it will be you saying when this is so, not anyone else.

And I'll be with you, by your side, with ideas, cues, methods, suggestions, things you already know and a universe of new opportunities. And remember, the one making the difference will be you.

6. TTM Is Focused on Objectives vs. GT Is Focused on Intention

What's the difference between an objective and an intention?

How is this question relevant with regard to the quality of your life?

Traditional time management is always about objectives. Guerrilla Time talks about intention in addition to dealing with objectives.

Some time ago, I coached two people of high standing in the financial world. Both of them contacted me (interestingly at about the same time) with plans to take a step from which there would have been no coming back. Despite the media's seeing them as remarkable examples of how to effectively reach goals in terms of career advances and money making, both of them were seriously thinking of putting an end to it all.

What a great opportunity for me, barely into my thirties, with a great desire to "advance my career" and "achieve success!"

I had two men in front of me, the essences of success, of whom outside observers would have said: "He's a success. WOW! Good for him!"

But the men themselves didn't see it this way.

Both of them had achieved extraordinary things in terms of work and money, showing themselves to be real professionals in defining and reaching goals. What they found out, right after reaching those goals, was that the things that they had strived for meant little to them or, better, that they weren't the only things that mattered, as indeed they had been for their whole lives up until that point.

Long before, they had learned the effectiveness of setting their goals in such a way as to allow them to move towards those goals. They had understood that voluntary and involuntary processes are active in each of us as we work towards well defined objectives. They understood the need for action and acted, on a daily basis, both with resolution and with commitment. And they had demonstrated, in the field, that they had made it, that they had reached their set objectives.

But this wasn't all they were looking for.

For one of them the objective was "to be rich". Someone, however, had told him that the objective was not specific enough. He was then required to specify how much money he wanted to earn and to set a time-frame for that goal. The objective, at that point, was clear and specific.

Too bad for him that no-one had said anything about intention. A simple question might have set his life upon a different course, more aligned to his deepest needs.

What's your intention for being rich? What's your intention for earning X in Y?

Had the intention been made clear, he may have discovered many ways to satisfy it. Perhaps one of them would have been the objective "to be rich". On the other hand, he may have realized—perhaps immediately, perhaps later (intentions and objectives being periodically refined and redefined)— that there was something else equally as important to him in life, something else to take into consideration. Something to give time to, to give energy and commitment to, thereby finding inner satisfaction and joy.

Alas, it hadn't been so. He had ridden fast, with the blinkers on, with no chance of enlightenment via the perspective of intention, without the choices that open up before us when we raise ourselves to the level of intention.

What a great lesson for me.

I struggle to express my satisfaction, so great it was, at seeing these two people rebloom from within, at each discovering his inner needs and bringing further talents to the fore, previously invisible talents which then became of great importance to him; my satisfaction at each revealing his human factor and becoming able to talk to himself using personal and professional development disciplines, not only dramatically improving the quality of his personal and professional life, but also allowing him to make up his mind about living, when another, darker, road had seemed his irredeemable fate.

This was an extremely useful experience for me.

Not having to wait years and, one can hope, not having to experience such a thing personally, to arrive at an understanding of how important are intention and the relationship we have with ourselves and our deepest needs.

From now on, I hope you won't orientate yourselves around objectives without previous investigation of your intention. Having discovered your intention, you should investigate the many ways it may be satisfied and which of those ways or combinations thereof is most suitable for the use of your energies and the living of your life.

7. TTM Is Mainly Based on Work Time vs. GT Is Based on Your Life

We've understood the importance of an inner guide (intention and objectives) and how these direct our attention and lead us to select our daily experiences.

So, what happens if we talk about objectives solely in terms of our work (as often is the case)?

We've seen the risks involved in not asking ourselves the question "What's my intention?"

But what do we risk by orientating ourselves exclusively around work?

I'm sure you already know the answer—we risk that our lives become nothing more than our work.

It may be your own choice. In that case, there's nothing to say on the matter. Freedom of choice is fundamental to a Guerrilla.

Too often, however, we are not dealing with a choice, but rather the fruit of habits we have not given ourselves permission to change or for whose changing we lack the tools.

While traditional time management is essentially focused on your job, Guerrilla Time is focused on you, on your life.

Guerrilla Time methods, tools and ideas are designed to be used in an all-round fashion. We are not job, family, hobbies or friends. We are much, much more.

And given the potency of focus, the power to direct our time, energy and attention along specific lines, it is useful to give ourselves time to understand the lines along which our focus might bring itself to bear.

Because, once direction is set—the flight path having been established, if you like—before you know it, you'll be on your way, powering along your chosen route.

So start from yourself. Start from your life. Make sure you take off in the right direction.

Work is undeniably an important factor for many. Yet we should consider work as part of the whole and not the whole itself, in that the whole may indeed turn out to be... nothing at all.

In the process of working out direction, pay close attention to your deepest needs, be sensitive to your emotions and use your logic effectively. Work, beholden to these effects, will struggle to dictate direction and will instead naturally accompany you on your adventure.

Guerrilla Time, too, will be by your side.

7+. TTM Is About Time vs. GT Is About Quality of Life

Exactly! Traditional time management is about time.

Guerrilla Time is about the quality of your life.

This is a huge difference, which you'll surely discover reading this book and above all in practice, practice, practice.

Chapter 3

MAKING TIME OUR PRECIOUS ALLY

Time

 it comfortably or, if you prefer, lie down.

Notice which parts of your body are relaxed and which ones less so.

Adjust your posture in order to be more at ease.

Set a timer to count down from 20 seconds (if you haven't got a timer, have someone count the seconds for you, on a watch or a clock).

As you start the timer, close your eyes and begin counting to 20 in your head.

When you reach 20 raise your hand and open your eyes.

Did you raise your hand before time or after time?

Or did you raise it exactly on the button?

Do it again. This time, do it standing up after a run. Then do it again, this time as you get up in the morning. Then again, and again, always changing the setting. What you'll discover is that time is subjective. Your hand might go up right on 20. It will certainly go up before or after the mark, and perhaps by a lot at times. If you do it with a group of friends, you'll see people raising hands seriously early and others doing so long after the objective twenty seconds have passed.

Time is subjective.

Having conducted your experiments, you will have discovered that time does not only change from person to person, but changes for the individual according to setting, one setting causing 20 seconds to be lived more or less swiftly than another setting. Our inner perception of time changes with regard to our psycho-physical-emotional state.

Time is subjective. Clock-time is not this kind of time. This kind of time is subjective time, which varies according to the way we feel.

All of us should be familiar with having to stand in line for a good slice of time. At the post office it's not uncommon. We arrive and there's the line. We wait, and we wait, and we wait. It seems an hour has passed. We glance at our watches. But can it be? That only ten little minutes have swung by? Change of scene. We're at party, having fun, talking about fancy things with fancy people, spying the characters in the crowd, dancing. We'd laugh if you told us we arrived 3 hours ago; surely it can't be more than one… But the watch tells us three, with a straight face.

All this happens *spontaneously*.

But what if we could do it on purpose? Perhaps *stretching* our pleasant experiences and *shrinking* our unpleasant ones.

What if we could alter our perception of time so as to have more when we need it or to make it pass more swiftly when life's a drag?

Several disciplines of both personal and professional development tell us that it's possible. They also have a name for the phenomenon: *time distortion*. With proper practice, time distortion can be mastered. Those of you interested in further reading should investigate Milton H. Erickson's work on the topic.

An interesting observation to commit to memory is the following: Our psycho-physical-emotional state heavily influences our perception of time. Since we are talking about Guerrilla Time, this is significant!

There's more.

Think of a few tough situations you've faced in your life. Situations you've had problems dealing with, yet which you were sure you were ready for, sure you knew enough to face. Despite your knowledge and preparation, you struggled… If you look back on these situations, you might see what they have in common.

Now, think of a few occasions when the best of you emerged, when your skills "spontaneously" surfaced in an effortless way; you were fully present and you responded successfully to the different challenges, surprising even yourself with all that you were able to do. Here, too, you might see what they have in common.

So what is it that links these experiences?

Exactly… it's your state!

In the former situations, it was an unsuitable state. In the latter, it was a state of grace.

One's psycho-physical-emotional state influences one's performance.

One of the fundamentals of Guerrilla Time is being able to choose that state. I'll provide you with some useful tools to make these choices at least partly accessible through experience.

Guerrillas don't want to be victims of their states. They want to be able to choose them. They want to affect their own performance so as to be aligned with their own intentions. They also want to increase the value of their talents and they know that their state is key to doing that.

As I've said, Guerrilla Time focuses on the human factor—and state is a key aspect of that.

Alibis that Prevent Us from Improving

On the temple of the Oracle in Delphi we read: "Know Thyself" (words yet to be unanimously attributed to a particular author, just for the record).

I recently met with a friend who told me how much he would have loved to learn French. He added "But I haven't got time."

An alibi.

A Guerrilla for whom something is very important always finds time for that thing.

It's way too easy to say "I haven't got time". People look at you and seem to say "I see". And you feel justified. Justified not to do, not to act, not to find solutions.

What you're actually saying is "It's not that important to me".

If it were really important, how could you not find time for it?

What you're holding in your hands is the right book. Keep on reading.

When some people are offered the chance to change (for the better, of course), they come up with excuses, besides the famous "I haven't got time".

They're like the fly that won't leave the house, no matter how many windows you open, no matter how many times you swipe at it.

Something's bound to go wrong out there, beyond one of those windows. They know what to expect. Familiarity is king. Whatever the downsides to indoor living, better the devil you know than the devil you don't. Well, sometimes it's the devil you know that gets you in the end, perhaps trapping you between window pane and lace curtain in a tragic and futile last jig.

Familiarity with things gives us an illusory feeling of security. To know what's going to happen is reassuring. It must be an illusion, however, since it's not true that if you always do what you've always done you'll always get what you've always gotten. Imagine employees pulling into their usual parking spaces believing all to be well simply because they've performed the same maneuver for the past 6 years without a hitch. And what if half the road's been eaten up by diggers to fix the drains underneath? It's costly to drive into a hole in the road, not to mention silly.

The truth is, we don't know what the future will bring, period! The idea that familiarity will afford us security is not only absurd, but reduces the quality of our lives.

Is this what you want?

Guerrillas know how to smile at themselves when they realize they are inventing alibis. They know how unproductive alibis can be.

"One thing is theory, another is practice" is a line that might well be seen as appropriate in some traditional time management books. Not here though. Watch out! It's an alibi!

Guerrilla Time is action, clever action led by method.

But you have to make the best investment of your life (and your time), namely the careful reading of this book, acting upon and learning from the feedback you receive.

I'm with you.

I'll give you exercises to do, tools to use, methods to follow. But, once again, it will ultimately depend on you.

You might say "I'm particular" or, regarding your job, "my job's particular".

As every single raindrop is different from its fellows, each of us and each of our jobs is different one from the next.

Sure, it's true, each of us is particular, and it's precisely for this reason that Guerrilla Time is based on the human factor. Not just any old human factor, but a specific you human factor. You reading this page, you beginning to understand that it's you making the difference. I'll merely be facilitator, and then the ball's in your court. Even with your opponent weakened, you still need to connect racket to ball and send it sailing over the net to score the point!

And here you'll learn many ways to make that key shot.

Have you started to smile at yourself?

Have you started to take yourself a little less seriously?

Remember, being truly serious means at times being able to smile at yourself. Yes, that's right. Smiling at yourself can be more serious than having a serious attitude.

Once again, it's a matter of state!

Traps

Let's investigate further this *human factor*. Guerrillas of time do this continuously throughout their lives.

"Know thyself" represents one of the most fascinating and satisfying journeys we can make.

In the mid-sixties, American researchers Robert Rosenthal and Lenore Jacobson conducted an experiment at an elementary school in California. Pupils were first made to do an intelligence test. Then, entirely at random and without looking at the test results, Rosenthal and Jacobson selected a limited number of children and informed the teachers that those children were very intelligent.

A year later, the two researchers returned to the school and noticed that the randomly selected children had remarkably improved their scholastic performance, becoming the best in their classes. Incredible, isn't it?

The positive influence of teachers, who believed these children to be the most gifted, had stimulated them to such a degree as to make them outperform all others in their classes.

Here the effect was positive, but it's easy to imagine the other side of the coin.

This effect is known as the Pygmalion effect and, in addition to scholastic environments, it appears in relationships between managers and the employees in their charge, between parents and their children and in every context in which social relationships develop.

Expectations can strongly influence the quality of interpersonal relationships and the performance of those subject to the expectations.

We're dealing with "self-fulfilling prophecies".

Careful: Prophecies made about other people are not the only ones that have strong influence.

There are the prophecies we make about ourselves too.

The following claim can help us to think critically about the issue:

"Whether you think you can do something or you think you can't, you're right."

This sentence is offered up by traditional time management in support of the following rationale: Believing you can, and thus acting in all respects as if you could, is the key to doing something and especially to doing it well. Believing you can't, and again acting accordingly, you won't be up to the task and at the very least you won't be able to do the thing well. In other words, the claim is that a prophecy about oneself will always be self-fulfilling.

Well, if we think we won't be able to do something, most of the time the result is inaction. We sit around and wait (not really choosing to wait, which is to say that waiting, as a real choice, can be wise and appropriate with regard to our objectives).

And believing that we can't, it's rather likely that we won't, in that success depends on action towards success and, believing success impossible, we don't act towards it.

In the end, we say "I knew I couldn't do it". Our belief was not only correct, but also the cause of its correctness.

And so begins a vicious circle of defeat.

Looking at the positive side of the equation, if we believe we can do something, we start to act towards success. It may take some time before our action moves us towards success, but sooner or later it will happen. We'll learn what needs to be done, which direction to take for this "can" to become an accurate prophecy. We'll become swifter and wiser and we'll learn from experience. In the end we may not achieve our goal, but think how much we'll learn on the way!

Perhaps next time it'll be different.

The basic question is: How much did you learn?

So the current result doesn't satisfy you. Fine, you'll be able to act accordingly, to change your strategies, to acquire new tools.

"There is no failure, only feedback."

And there's no better learning than experience.

Here's a suggestion: Enjoy the experience of learning.

In every single moment of your life you can learn something new.

Nothing that surrounds you, no environment or collection of things in the world, remains unaltered from one moment to the next. Every instant something changes. If we have blindfolds over our eyes and plugs in our ears, we see only those things which are no longer there, we hear sounds long gone and we no longer live the fantastic experience of the *here and now*, where everything is continuously becoming.

Look at the people in your immediate space. Look again and they'll have changed. Inevitably we change, from one moment to the next.

When you look in a mirror, you change before your very eyes.

The question is: How do you want to change?

At times familiarity is what we seek and familiarity betrays us. It makes things which are different one from the next appear to us the same, unaltered over time, as if the inevitable were not so inevitable. And therefore we don't act according to our current experience, but rather as if we were faced with the past. Yet no matter how well we can face the past, surely we are not facing the present well. We are living in another temporal dimension, responding to sounds, images and feelings from the past.

Guerrillas know how to live in the present, how to appreciate every moment, even the tough ones, seizing upon and enjoying change, seeing the differences and loving challenges, leaving their comfort zones. They also love to interact with people in the here and now. And by "interact with people", I also mean the interactions each Guerrilla has with him/herself.

Guerrillas also learn something fundamental: how to choose their own states.

Sure, they can enjoy memories of the past, they can hypothesize possible futures, but they can also choose to experience the reality and richness of the present moment.

They know how to give themselves direction and how to investigate intention; they make sure objectives are aligned with intention and they love to enjoy the adventure of the here and now in a dynamic and vital way.

But how is all this possible?

The question is *how*, not *if*.

Indeed, it *is* possible. It *can* be done.

Knowing it to be so, we should arm ourselves with effective methods and tools and these should take the human factor into account.

Ignorance can be very expensive. And not merely in monetary terms. This is a question of quality of life. Something we mustn't forget.

As you're reading, how do you feel?

Do you feel you can do it? Will you commit yourself to action?

If the answer to the second question is a strong yes you can skip directly to the next chapter.

If you still have some doubts, keep reading.

If you have conflicting feelings, don't deny them. Here, being first in the class means nothing. Here, there's you and only you. And you always come first!

Accept the feelings that come, they're your hidden gold; they tell you there's something important to be considered!

You're lucky, you know. You're still sensitive enough to feel your body, to perceive it. Others have learned to ignore the signals from their bodies, with disastrous consequences for them.

There's a great risk, which must be offset with the use of the right tools. It's the risk of self-sabotage, whereby our own efforts are sabotaged by our own hands, and not by the context and not by the hands of others. It's us.

Those who have chosen (unfortunately) to ignore the signals coming from their bodies often finds themselves in this situation, as if driving with the handbrake on! It's a real struggle. Lots of energy gets wasted, the engine striving away while the brakes hold the car still. The gas runs out and the car hasn't moved.

And we are much, much more than a car.

Rather than considering these signals a bother, consider them allies, messengers that enable you to find better solutions, messengers that might invite you to apply intelligent changes to the strategies you've discovered, messengers that allow you to discover your deepest needs and to act so as to satisfy them.

And once you've done this, the strength, coherence and congruence with which you will pursue your intentions and achieve your objectives will be simply incredible. Your psycho-physical-emotional state will be excellent and results will come your way. You will become a Guerrilla, often surprising yourself by how much you can do.

Getting Past Procrastination

What happens when people unerringly procrastinate?

Do you think they achieve their objectives, that they satisfy their intentions? They don't.

Tomorrow might in fact not be another day.

If you find yourself procrastinating and this is not your choice, I have for you some simple and important observations that can help.

Better to Do Something Good Than Not Do Something Excellent

Before I started to write books, I saw writing as a serious issue. I still see it that way. But thinking of writing as something serious, I thought a book had to be perfect before being published. Really, perfect! Can you imagine the result of such thinking? Many secret dreams and no published book!

Someone brought it to my attention that I was depriving those interested of what I had to say and to share, of things really important to them (thanks Jay). It made me think, and yet it wasn't enough. I had a strong alibi: "I haven't got time."

Then I met a friend with the same alibi. I still remember how we laughed...
at ourselves!

To laugh at yourself, what an opportunity!

We gave ourselves a challenge—who could write the worst book in the
least time. That's how I came to write my first book (it's not this one!). The
book was not bad at all; simply, it wasn't perfect!

I was still unsatisfied. I could have improved it. But it was there,
written, ready.

And I published it.

And then an extraordinary thing happened. People read it, quoted it, used
it as a guide, even though it wasn't perfect!

That led the way to other adventures, one of which you are holding in
your hands.

You Cannot Learn Without Making Mistakes

Having had the opportunity to observe children growing up, I find it interesting
how certain cultures want people to learn without making mistakes. Yep, no
mistakes whatsoever.

So what does the word *mistake* mean?

First of all, it's only a word (an image for those who read it, a sound for
those who hear it). And, as with every other word, it has no meaning until we
give one to it. And meaning is given by how we experience the word, how it
makes us feel and the emotions linked to it.

Do you feel uneasy when you hear the word *mistake*?

Do you freeze up, get stuck?

If you are about to start something new, does it help you learn?

Your psycho-physical-emotional state influences your actions, behaviors
and performance in a very strong way.

Let's replace *mistake* with *feedback*, in fact a much more appropriate word.

We are "fed" by the experience we have interacting with the world. It's the
Holy Grail of learning.

Feedback is just feedback.

Imagine you have an intention and what you are doing is not leading you where you want to go. If your sensory experience is telling you this, you simply do something else.

You just do what every great learner does—you define intention and objectives, act and… receive the feedback. If what you are doing is not leading you where you want to go, you do something else.

Very simple.

I remember watching my son experimenting with a VCR. One day he had decided that the weird thing in the corner of the room needed his attention. He picks up a videocassette and waddles over to the "thing"… crashing against it. Over and over the cassette crashes against the player. I have to hold myself back. I'm tempted to show him, to give him the direct route to success. But alone he's getting there. With every attempt he tries something… he's learning.

An adult might have given up. Too many mistakes.

But a child doesn't know what a mistake is. He experiences things and is fed by experience.

Some think the task of parents is to ensure children learn without negative consequences.

Hooray for this ignorance!

The child keeps trying and testing, until the "right" move is made and the child becomes his/her parents' pride and joy.

Actually all attempts are "right".

Gaining an understanding of things, namely learning, is a challenge. And children do better than adults in this sphere.

And if there is no "mistake", all we have is feedback.

If you have a mistake phobia, prescribe yourself a mistake!

Today I have to make at least… x mistakes.

Remember, many great discoveries come from "mistakes". People have been moving in a particular direction and while some complained about the lack of results others realized these individuals had discovered something new, something totally unexpected, not aligned with the original intention or objectives.

This is exactly what happened with Viagra.

In 1986, at Pfizer Central Research in Sandwich in the UK, researchers discovered that inhibiting the PDE5 enzyme in the non-striated part of muscles decreases vascular resistance and reduces the aggregation of blood platelets, responsible for blood-clotting, high concentrations of which in veins or arteries can cause partial or total obstruction.

Researchers thought of a beneficial effect of PDE5 on angina pectoris. It might prevent obstruction of coronary arteries, the cause of myocardial infarction, or heart attacks in common speech. Three years of testing turned up unsatisfactory results, but researchers witnessed an interesting phenomenon.

There were side effects. Some realized that one of these, very much undesired by the initial research, was actually what a lot of people longed for!

Hence the creation of one the world's most used drugs, now having nothing to do with angina pectoris (which can be tackled rather more effectively without Viagra!).

Think how many important discoveries you might make by treating a mistake as simple feedback; perhaps discovers so remarkable as to take you totally by surprise.

The Intention Behind Procrastination

Investigating the intention behind objectives is fundamental.

So what if we used the magic "intention question" to overcome procrastination?

If you constantly procrastinate, ask yourself:

What's the intention behind my procrastination?

Before answering I suggest you sleep on it.

We want an inner response, not a rational analysis.

You may discover that the intention is indeed positive and that procrastination is a way to satisfy it. There are several other ways which don't have the unpleasant side effects of procrastination, side effects such as feelings of apathy, feeling useless, feeling impotent or feeling dissatisfied.

How many other ways are there, besides procrastination, that fulfill your personal satisfaction, that give you a sense of self-effectiveness and that make you aware that you're going in the right direction?

Once you've found the alternatives to satisfy the intention, put them into practice… enjoy the results and notice those that work best for you. You might end up upon hitherto untrodden pathways.

What happens if what you've found is not completely satisfying?

Learn from feedback and develop new ways of applying or combining the alternatives so as to understand which is the best possible experience for you.

Be careful, there may be several intentions.

Good luck.

And get ready to say a final goodbye to unintentional procrastination.

Find an "Accountability Partner"

Find one person (or more) who shares your firm intention to become a Guerrilla of Time. Ask your fellow aspirant to be your "accountability partner" (you can do the same for him or her).

State your intentions and your goals, outline your strategy and summarize the situation with your accountability partner at regular intervals. Define and respect these intervals.

In addition to doing so with your accountability partner, you can state your intentions and goals to the people you care about.

Then see what happens.

And…

The above is not a complete list of solutions to procrastination.

I invite you to explore and to find "customized ways" so that you start to act and to go where you want to go.

And remember, if you want to go all around the world, start with a first step, then a second, then a third…

CHAPTER 4

17 SECRETS OF GUERRILLA TIME

1. YOU

xactly!

This book was written for you.

This book is designed for you.

This book is meant for you.

I trust you.

I trust your skills and potential.

I know there's genius inside of you, even if you've never been told so or if you think differently.

I know how to look beyond this.

I know you have plenty of hidden talents that are waiting to emerge and to be put into action to your advantage.

Keep discovering yourself, be curious about "know(ing) thyself," save some time for yourself.

If you save time for yourself, you will have more time for others, not to mention more time of higher quality.

Always remember, it's you that makes the difference. You can do it.

27

You'll discover many things on this journey.

Enjoy your path.

I wish you good exploration and brilliant action.

2. Personal Metaphor

If I asked you to describe yourself metaphorically in this moment, how would you describe yourself?

You can choose whichever metaphor comes to mind. Metaphors are just metaphors and it's *you* who'll discover the one that's best for you.

It might be a visual metaphor, one related to sound, perhaps one composed of feelings, tastes or smells; it might be a metaphor made out of words alone or it might be a metaphor which combines all of the above.

Ask yourself the following:

Which metaphor might best describe me now?

Let the metaphor emerge spontaneously.

Wait and trust that, even in an unexpected moment, the metaphor will emerge from within.

It is only a matter of time. And as you wait you can do something else and enjoy doing that thing; the question will work away deep within you.

As soon as have your metaphor, thank yourself. Yes, thank yourself for having let it emerge. Something important happened inside of you.

Look at the metaphor, listen to it, experience it, taste it, smell it.

Do you like it?

Take your time and ask yourself the following questions (ask them when it feels right; it doesn't have to be now):

Does it satisfy my deepest wishes?

Does it help me achieve my objectives?

What are the positive consequences of this metaphor?

What are the negative consequences of this metaphor?

Let time pass. It's even better if you sleep on it.

Then…

Here's the most important question:

Which metaphor would you like for yourself?

It's essential that it comes from within, with absolutely no conscious effort.

It's crucial that you feel it as your own, that all your body feels fine as you think about it.

If it's not like that, let one that like that emerge, one that gives you an overall pleasant feeling.

No one else can tell you if this is the right metaphor for you.

You and you alone will know.

Only you, with your awareness of your feelings.

Metaphors strongly activate our involuntary processes, the motors of change.

A metaphor has a power beyond words.

Even your intuitions can take the shape of a metaphor.

We also invite your deepest intentions to emerge as a metaphor.

There should be very little room for rationality in this process, and it has to be like that. We want to activate the non-dominant hemisphere, we want involuntary processes to be at the heart of the matter.

Give yourself all the time you need for this. We don't know how long it will take. Here, the time you need has absolutely no meaning.

The impact on your life will be remarkable.

Remember to note, every once in a while, if your metaphor still makes you feel fine and be ready to let a new one emerge should this no longer happen.

3. Quality of Life

In this book we talk about quality of life, not about "management" of time.

This is quality of life as *you* understand it, quality of life according to *your* meaning of the phrase.

The personal metaphor exercise will be of great help.

Paying attention to the feelings in your body, to all its sensations, will be your feedback for a remarkable adventure.

Take some time for yourself, find a quiet place and ask yourself:

What does quality of life mean to me?

You can start from your direct experiences, asking yourself:

How do I feel when I experience moments of high quality?

Let those feelings float, so that you can feel them in your body.

Now you have some "sensory based" references, you know what "quality of life" means in your body and if you are not satisfied with those feelings, keep looking. A word is always a word. But I want it to turn into a sensory-based experience and I want you to know when you experience what is verbally called "quality of life."

When you know what "quality of life" means to you and as you continue to search for what it can mean to you (in that what it means to you may constantly be redefined by experience) you will open doors to new opportunities to live your time in the way you want.

Set your rationality aside for a while and frame all of the responses to the questions you ask yourself as images, sounds, feelings, smells and tastes. These constitute our primary experience.

Let language come after.

A Guerrilla knows language is an extraordinary tool but sometimes it's better to live a sensory-based experience with no verbal content.

It doesn't matter if you can't verbally answer your questions, it's ok… fully live your experience.

Many high quality things cannot be expressed in words!

4. Dynamic Balancing

Walk 5 normal steps forward, then come back.

Again, 5 normal steps forward, then back again.

This time, walk much slower and, after coming back, repeat the exercise over and over, slower and slower.

Take time for this exercise and then keep reading.

You'll soon notice that your gait is a continuous, dynamic balancing act that allows you to stay in balance as you walk.

Guerrillas of Time know how to balance like this in life, according to their needs, even their deepest ones.

Guerrillas know that there are endless ways to live their time, some of which may be in mutual opposition. A Guerrilla knows balance is not static, but dynamic.

A Guerrilla knows that dynamic balancing needs constant adjustment, presence, the capacity to notice what's going on without and within, the flexibility to modify one's behavior when it's not aligned with intention and objectives, the sensitivity to notice one's likes and dislikes, to feel one's own needs.

Guerrillas know that the sun always shines behind the clouds and they know where to find shelter from a storm, even when they decide to stay under the rain and get soaked.

A Guerrilla knows the certainty of being is an illusion and enjoys the becoming.

5. Intention

Intention is a lighthouse that guides and directs us in the dark.

Intention directs our attention and our life in ways that elude a precise rational description.

Intention deeply influences us.

Intention is a way to escape the cage of our behaviors. We can discover other behaviors. Once we discover the intention behind a behavior, we can discover many other more effective behaviors to satisfy the intention.

Intention opens the door to new choices.

A friend of mine kept fighting with his wife. When asked why, he would say:

"Because she said this, because she said that…"

The question why often leads to justifications, to thinking in a cause and effect manner, when the reality of human affairs is far more complex and based on influencing dynamics, not ones of cause and effect. Those seeking justifications or causes have no way to get rid of such slavery.

The question, "What is your intention?" brought my friend to silence. No longer justification, just a simple question: What do you want?

After defining the intention, it was much easier for him to find new ways to move in the desired direction, without the negative consequences of the old habits.

A Guerrilla knows how to clarify his or her intention, and does so by letting intention emerge from within.

Guerrillas know the power of intention; they know that attention is one of the most limited resources and therefore they direct it in the most appropriate way.

Guerrillas always ask themselves: What is my intention in doing what I am doing? They then assess the paths they are on and compare to the paths they want to be on.

6. Adventure

In this world there are people who live their lives in eternal wandering.

If it's their choice, it's ok. If not, the quality of their lives could be different. All it takes is to learn the art of planning.

In our world, there are people who want to plan everything.

Again, if it's their choice, it's ok. If not, the quality of their lives could be different. All it takes is to learn the art of living the moment and its experiences.

If wandering is your most likely behavior, you'll find many useful suggestions in this book. Don't forget the power of your personal metaphor, of intention and objectives.

If you tend to plan everything… welcome.

A recent operative study in the field of professional work showed that 50% of work time is consumed dealing with unexpected events.

This percentage has increased in recent times, as economic and social scenarios mutate far quicker than they used to.

A high degree of entropy seems to be part of our days.

This is a real tragedy for those who want to plan everything. Every day the agenda will be turned upside down. Frustration, anger and tension may well result.

With consequences you can easily imagine.

By now, you're well aware that one's psycho-physical-emotional state strongly influences one's behavior.

An easy exit from this negative spiral, and the first thing to try, is to plan some time for unexpected events.

Keep back x amount of time to face unexpected events effectively, factoring it into your agenda. Perhaps this sounds familiar.

So let's now investigate something a lot less familiar.

What would it be like being able to live well without planning?

I'm not suggesting living by the day, or moment-to-moment for that matter.

Rather, I'm suggesting that we acquire the ability to do so.

For those who plan everything, this isn't a choice at hand; it's something inaccessible.

So let's proceed one step at a time, taking habits into account as part of the human factor.

With no particular goal in mind, start setting aside 10 minutes of your time every 2 days for doing exactly what you want to do in those 10 minutes. In those 10 minutes, pay attention to the signals from your body; be sensitive to them. This may not be easy for some people.

In their everyday lives, they experience certain psycho-physical-emotional states which do not encourage sensitivity to their bodies and its internal changes.

If it is too complicated for you to feel your body, start to introduce some awareness exercises in your daily practice. You'll find a few in this book.

Why is having this ability so important? Because it allows you to be sensitive to your most inner needs and to take them into account in the adventure of living, so as to progressively augment the quality of your life.

Once you have the choice to enter a state of bodily awareness, what is it that increases satisfaction and pleasure and what is it that does not in those 10 minutes?

Be careful: You're outside your comfort zone, so tolerate this initial feeling of healthy confusion or similar feelings that aren't always so pleasant. You're exploring new possibilities and every new journey, especially for creatures of habit, may at the very beginning imply a little effort or sacrifice. After a while, such feelings will fade away and new, pleasant ones, which will lead you in those 10 minutes, will emerge.

It's worth it, believe me.

As you start enjoying your ten minutes, increase the frequency of this exercise and do it day in, day out. Ten minutes all for yourself, for your most intimate and urgent needs.

WOW!

You may decide to increase the length of time you give yourself—it's a new choice.

After a while, dynamic balancing, alternation between direction and adventure, living the here and now and enjoying the moment will all become extremely meaningful to you.

I wish you all good exploration.

7. Subjectivity

Perception of time is subjective. It's as subjective as the way you make all this a part of your daily life. After practicing, practicing, practicing, ideas, tools and methods will become new, real choices and lots of new opportunities will unfold before you, letting you to live the life you want.

Time is subjective.

Using social media, I asked people to help me enrich this book and... for me the unimaginable happened. Further prove that the unexpected is to be enjoyed.

All the people who replied wrote their own metaphors of time, consciously or unconsciously.

Stories have always had a strong hold on us. Think of fairy tales, movies, serials, books.

A world of metaphors.

Metaphors impact directly on our involuntary processes, influence the way we look at things, the way we listen, feel, smell and taste the world. They influence our experience.

Imagine the impact your metaphor of time could have.

Create your metaphor of time.

Let it come from within, as every other metaphor we talked about.

It can be composed of images, sounds, feelings, smells, tastes or words.

If it's in words, write it down. If it has a different form, represent it somehow.

It might be a long metaphor or a short one.

Consider the following verbal metaphors:

"Time is never enough."

Or

"There's never time to do the things we like."

Or, as someone wrote:

"It's useless to fight against time, to challenge it or to complain about wasted time. Time will always win!"

What are the consequences for a person who keeps thinking and processing this way?

In this book I say that the way you live your life, the way you live your time, is a choice that you can have at hand.

My intention is to establish the setting for this choice to become part of your life.

If this is also your intention, then the question is:

Is your metaphor of time satisfying this intention?

In other words:

Does it support your choice to live your time in the way you really want to?

If so, great. Your metaphor is a good guide. Perhaps you were already aware of it. Perhaps you discovered it during the exercise.

Be sensitive to changes in the metaphor, bearing in mind that a metaphor is only a metaphor; this metaphor is your own metaphor and you are the main character in it.

If you decide to change and modify it, be sensitive to your body and the feedback it gives you.

If the answer is no, your current metaphor of time is not helping your choice to live your life the way you want, ask yourself the following:

Which metaphor of time might help me to fully satisfy my intention, allowing me to live a life of higher quality?

Remember not to answer at once; let the question stimulate choices from deep inside.

8. Learning from Your Experiences

Our culture often proposes the following message: Ask a master, someone "who knows better", which way to go.

What if you were that master?

Or, humbly, if you became that master?

The purpose of this book is to give you ideas, suggestions, methods, tools and metaphors for you to become master of your own time.

It's a great challenge, which calls many well rooted beliefs into question, on both conscious and unconscious levels.

I've insisted on your paying attention to your feelings.

I've insisted on your experiencing things.

I've insisted that you practice, that you step into action.

And you've fully understood the value of feedback from your experience.

Learning from your needs, that's what I suggest.

The way of a master, *par excellence.*

As your traveling companion, I want to tell you about something that might be very useful.

I learned to play tennis by trial and error and by watching other people play, who weren't much good either! I would get a few balls over the net and I enjoyed mixed fortunes at the occasional tournaments I played.

After a few years of playing the sport, I began to feel a pain in my right shoulder about half an hour into training or into a match, especially when I hit a backhand.

So I sought advice from a trainer. It was hard, because I was one of those stubborn types who want to do everything by themselves.

Getting advice with me was a novice to the sport.

Who do you suppose first learned to hit the ball as the trainer demonstrated?

That's right. The new guy!

My swing had become a part of me. I had to start anew, to develop a new swing which would improve my backhand and get rid of the pain, whether in training or a match. In other words, a way of moving unlike the one employed to date.

The trainer was a cunning teacher. He didn't teach you the "right" move, but carefully observed you and let you learn in your own way.

Nevertheless, the newbie was still better than me.

By the time of the next match, my frustration had increased. First among reasons for this was my inability to put into practice what I had learned from my trainer. On the court, facing the opponent, it just didn't engage. The second among my woes was that now I couldn't even do what I could do before (namely, send the ball over the net). Last but not least, my pain was ever present during play.

I thought about giving up on the lessons.

However, the pain was unbearable and I still desperately wanted to play tennis, so I kept taking them.

On one occasion, the day before a scheduled lesson, I took a trip to the mountains.

Walking along one of the main tracks, the going easy and all around peaceful and calm, I, with my walking companions, came at length upon a lodge, which was undergoing maintenance. The silence broken and the view somewhat spoiled by the noisy and sprawling construction-works, we noticed a track, away to our right, punctuated with hanging boughs and rowdy nature's other attempts to hide the path from sight. Definitely not a well-trodden highway. We decided to take it—all of a sudden struck by a strong desire to explore.

After some arduous minutes and a few tears to our shirts, we emerged into one of the most beautiful valleys I had ever seen, arrayed with no more than the purest sounds of nature, the crispest rays of sunlight and a faint Moon peering down from the bluest of backdrops.

WOW!

Words can only suggest this marvel to you!

We told friends about it—"Go and see that place, it's so…er…wow!" What real word could describe it? After staying in the valley for a while, we made our way back towards the main track. Once passed the lodge and its ugly chaos, we realized that the small path leading down to the valley had grown into something far bigger for us than the main track was now. The main track, perfectly pleasant not so long ago, was now a different thing.

And from there back to tennis. With the trainer, I now practiced and used my new swing over and over, making it my own and paying attention to the feelings my body was giving rise to.

It was tiring, but I had a different awareness.

By the end of the lesson I had set up a practice schedule, a real action plan.

About a month later, a friend with whom I was playing a game made me aware of something. The swing I was using for my backhand was the new one, efficient and effective as never before. And no pain in more than two hours!

Guerrillas know that before turning a new practice into a real choice we need to practice, practice, practice.

Only then can we really choose.

9. Learning from Other People's Experiences

Our lives are too short to learn everything by trial and error, although sometimes there's no other way.

This book wants to help you become a Guerrilla of time, a master of your time.

This books gives you the basics. You'll learn the ropes.

When you have the base, the rest comes easy.

A Guerrilla of time knows how valuable it is to carefully watch and listen to those who already have remarkable results.

What great resources other people's experiences are!

Be curious, look around, you can find inspiration to improve the quality of your life everywhere.

Remember, however, to assess what you learn from other people according to your own experience. It's you that makes the difference. What works for you works for you.

Put what you see and hear into practice, give it time to become another choice at your disposal and, when it has, choose for the better.

Remember, nothing can replace your experience.

10. Passion

Guerrillas of time feed their time with passion.

They do it by choosing things that fascinate them or by engaging while learning new things.

Passion can nurture the great feats of our lives and living a life of high quality is a feat of the greatest value.

Passion is passed on. Passionate people excite, encourage and stimulate other people.

Passion can make impossible things possible.

A group of passionate people can make remarkable changes.

Passion for life, for life's gifts in every moment, even in the most apparently meaningless moments, casts a new light, allows new opportunities to unfold, opens new doors wide.

With passion, effort become commitment and commitment is fed by satisfaction and joy.

How many different ways do you know to live your passion?

How can you turn your life into a great adventure for you and the people around you?

Guerrillas remember to ask themselves such questions often... letting answers come from within, feeding their lives with passion.

11. Satisfaction

We often hear about *saved* time.

"With this technique, I could save myself 20 minutes in my day."

Congratulations! What are you going to do with those twenty minutes?

How do you live the other hours, just to save those 20 minutes?

With what result?

With what kind of satisfaction?

My goal is not simply to save you time. My goal, for as long it's yours too, is to have you live your time with greater quality and satisfaction.

If the focus of your attention is solely on *saving* time, you'll loose sight of other very important aspects: I've already stressed the power of intention and objectives.

Ask yourself: How can I be more satisfied with my day?

Think of, for example, the time spent doing your tasks—think about the satisfaction coming from them.

The more you are satisfied, the better your psycho-physical-emotional state will be, the more efficiently and effectively you'll behavior, the higher the quality of your time will be and, therefore, the better the quality of your life.

Remember to ask yourself: Where am I focusing my attention?

12. Value

The value of time is a very important aspect for a Guerrilla of time.

Some say: Time is money.

These some are making a big mistake when they say this.

Time is life.

Giving our time value means living the life we want to live, giving our time, energy and attention to what best gives value to us.

You have to decide what *value* means to you.

In fact, it helps to give the word a good few meanings. Don't limit yourself to the economic sense (what allows me to earn the most): incorporate passion (what you like), satisfaction (what satisfies you) and added value (things you can do that others can't and that can give you and those around you an added value). The list is representative. Just add what's important to you.

When you consider the most relevant aspects of value, you'll begin to focus one of the most limited resources you have—your attention—in the desired direction.

13. Organization

Guerrillas of time know personal organization is time well spent.

They also know that their psycho-physical-emotional state is the key to organizing themselves.

Many people think organization is a waste of time or that it takes something away from action.

I remind them that a fly that keeps banging against a window pane is acting.

Too many people get organized when they are mighty tired because they had other and more important things to do when they weren't.

I remind them that when you're exhausted, it's time to rest, and it's definitely not the moment for doing strategic things.

A Guerrilla of time knows action is enlightened by organization.

A Guerrilla of time, while getting organized, knows how important it is to clarify intention and objectives, to make an action plan, to factor in time for unexpected things.

A Guerrilla of time knows how important it is to check things through feelings, how important it is to act aligned with one's self and how powerful it is when reason and feelings are on the same page.

Before getting organized, remember to always check your psycho-physical-emotional state; if it's not the most suitable state, change it or do something else.

Simple things may work very well:

- take a walk;
- start breathing rhythmically using your abdomen (sometimes, in productive states, we forget about breathing and breathe shallowly or in a strange way);
- relax.

Never give less than your full attention to planning in an optimum psycho-physical-emotional state.

(For those who think this may become an alibi for not getting organized: read "a good psycho-physical-emotional state" rather than "an optimum psycho-physical-emotional state").

14. Monitoring

Carefully monitor your plan as you act.

Ask yourself:

Is it really what I want?

Summarizing and checking your intention and your objectives are essential in order to be where you want to be and not elsewhere. Give yourself due time—speeding away in the undesired direction takes us further away from our goal.

If the answer is *yes*, ask yourself, one question at a time:

Is this the most appropriate way to achieve it?

Are there various ways to satisfy my intention, and which might improve the effectiveness of my plan?

How can I make my plan more efficient and effective and at the same time give my time its proper value?

Keep eyes and ears open, be sensitive to your feelings.

Constant monitoring allows you to be enriched by feedback from the actions that follow in your plan.

Be aware, those who don't monitor are akin to a blindfolded fighter pilot. A Guerrilla knows a plan is nothing without assessment via experience.

15. Flexibility

"If that doesn't work, do something else."

Given intention, flexibility allows you to proceed in the desired direction, to take into account what actually happens and to respond effectively.

We may plan very well, but we can't be oracles and nor can we predict the future. If you actually can, please give me a call!

When flying towards a particular destination, an airplane that detects turbulence ahead might change route to reach the same destination.

Rarely, if things are really bad at the desired destination, the plane switches destination, ensuring the safety of passengers and crew (the intention).

Flexibility in uncertain and dynamic contexts is key, as is understanding where we are going, with our senses switched on, noting if our route is taking us in the desired direction or not.

Flexibility doesn't come naturally for many adults. We have to learn it.

If you catch yourself saying: "It's a question of personality, I'm not like that," you're making a terrible mistake—you're confused between what you are and what you do (i.e. your current behaviors and the skills you currently put to use in the field). In fact, you are much, much more than what you do!

Using the right tools, disciplined practice and commitment, your behaviors can change in such a way as to make you say about how you used to think

"Sometimes we really do have a lot of nonsense in our heads."

Ask yourself the questions which make you seek out new ways, new solutions, new opportunities. For example:

How can I learn to be more flexible?

Or

How can I improve my ability to understand that I am heading in the right direction?

Watch out for *well-meaning souls*—think of all the graves that have been filled in the name of noble causes—who may mistake flexibility for a lack of coherence. They tell you that what you are doing doesn't fit with who you are, taking your behavior to be you.

But you are much, much more than what you do in a particular moment.

Given your deepest intentions—and herein lies your coherence—flexibility allows you to reach your objectives in a much easier way, fully respecting yourself and the people around you.

Guerrillas know how important flexibility is if they are to satisfy intentions and achieve objectives. They also know how important it is to have an ethical compass which points to the humanity of human beings.

16. State

A famous anthropologist from the last century would often recount the following aphorism:

"If you kick a ball, a physicist can tell you exactly where it will fall. If you kick a rat, he can't." [Author's note: the animal in this case is not the one featuring in the original aphorism]

Cause-effect logic, a normal thing in relationships between animals and things, doesn't apply between animals and animals.

The bad news is, many a time, we behave as if we're about to kick a ball.

Someone flicks a switch and the lights go out.

"You annoyed me."

"It made me feel bad."

These are examples of cause-effect logic, erroneously applied to humans.

The consequence of all this is:

We cease to be the protagonists in our lives and, worse, we become the victims.

If it's true that our psycho-physical-emotional state heavily influences our behavior and if it's true that this state is determined by factors outside of our influence, then we are not responsible for our actions.

This is the extreme consequence.

We undermine the concept of responsibility, understood as the capacity to act.

And we justify all behavior.

We become victims.

Luckily, for most people this only happens in rare and specific situations, even though we often tend to think in this way.

And the consequence?

A dramatic decrease in the quality of life.

If you want to improve the quality of your life, if you want to become the noblest of human beings, turn the ball back into a human being, with many choices at hand, in spite of influences from your environment and people all around you.

Guerrillas of time know how to accept influences that lead them in the desired direction. They are also able to be play the lead when things or people influence them to go in unwanted directions.

They know how to go against the mainstream when that is the desired direction. They trust their intuitions and senses, at the same time taking feedback from the outside world into due consideration.

They can do this thanks to a strong key skill. They are able to choose their psycho-physical-emotional state, not an easy task in such situations, yet definitely possible.

And worth it.

17. Action, Action, Action

All that I've told you will acquire value solely on one condition: that you, who are passionately reading this book, act.

Action, action, action.

Practice, practice, practice.

Have you started acting already?

Many important things have already been said by me and read by you. They're ready to be used, now.

If you've started acting, you're on the right road. Always find new ways during your day to apply what you're learning.

If you haven't started acting, no excuses, start doing so now.

Stop reading, go back and start doing it.

Be active as you read this book. Take notes, insert bookmarks on useful pages, chapters and sentences, underline what you'll put into practice. And then act!

I assure you that what you are reading is highly effective.

But only if you put it into practice and act, act and act.

Actions will be enlightened by method, corrected by feedback from yourself, by people around you and by your environment.

Keep your eyes and ears wide open and opportunities will come in unexpected moments. You'll be sensitive to your perceptions and to your deepest needs.

Many people love knowledge.

But it's important to join knowledge, the *I've understood*, to action. You won't be able to say that you've truly understood what's written in this book if you don't act.

And at each new reading, the concepts, methods and suggestions herein will take on a new light and a deeper understanding will become part of your personal wealth for the rest of your life. Above all, new opportunities for a better life will unfold before you.

How would you like to make your life amazing?

It's all here, in your hands.

Practice, practice, practice.

And thanks to your actions, what you have in your hands will turn into a life experience of the highest quality, day after day.

CHAPTER 5

DEVELOPING A GUERRILLA TIME PLAN

T he pages you've read so far contain many suggestions and things to be practiced that will allow you to gradually improve the quality of your life. You've read these pages, you've practiced the things to be practiced and they've become a part of you.

And if you haven't started practicing yet, I suggest you begin right now.

If curiosity for what I'm about to tell you is stronger, read on. There's only one condition: You have to promise yourself that you'll put every piece of advice into practice. As soon as you read it.

I've introduced topics in different ways, in order to involve your rational side and to influence you at a deeper level. This book is structured for its information to fall on fertile ground, bearing fruit in the form of actions that have the power to change your life.

Time's come to put things in order, to illuminate our action with the Guerrilla Time Plan.

I promised a simple and effective method. You'll also have more than 150 weapons at hand to improve the quality of your life.

A Guerrilla of time knows how important it is to start out on the right foot.

Starting out on the right foot means having a simple and effective 7 step plan.

The steps are as follows:

1. Developing the Guerrilla Time attitude
2. Learning about Guerrilla Time competitive advantage: the human factor
3. Learning to use Guerrilla Time weapons
4. Action plan
5. Action, action, action
6. Monitoring and feedback
7. Improvements

1. Developing the Guerrilla Time Attitude

How many people around the world think "I'm like this, this is who I am."

They have their "personality", their way of being, and this, and that, and so on.

Thus is their justification for whatever happens to them, for whatever they do.

What's the intention here?

Some do it for reasons of self-acceptance.

I accept myself for who I am. And this is a good intention.

But in what way does accepting yourself entail standing still, not acting so as to become yet more of what you want to be or, put another way, so as to change in accord with your desired direction?

In only a year, 98% of the atoms in your body are replaced by new ones. Being "the same" takes on a whole new meaning when we think about it this way.

In fact, when framed in such a way, the whole enterprise of remaining the same takes on an air of mission impossible. Action hero or no, it's a tough ask.

And yet many people believe that they do remain the same. You know why? They don't accept themselves.

Acceptance means accepting the fact that we constantly change and evolve, that we constantly undergo modification.

The thing to decide is: In which direction do we change, evolve and modify?

If we don't make up our own minds on the matter, something or someone else will!

Guerrillas know that they can improve. They deeply and completely accept this fact. They enjoy the here and now, whatever it is, even when aiming for better things.

Even when washing dishes, packing bags, cleaning the house—things we can't stand perhaps—we can find the positive side to each experience. Think of children, for whom every experience is a new one, including those we'd call banal. Every event brings a surprise, a WOW. Every moment is different. We can always learn something. Sometimes it's not easy. But we can.

And there's more.

We enjoy the here and now. And we settle on where we want to go.

We focus our attention on the things we want to happen.

We create the personal metaphor that makes us feel fine, that motivates us without making fun of us. After all, it's made for us. We created it, causing it to emerge from the inside out…and not by means of a rational effort to appear as this, that or the other…

This, that or the other can be stereotypes that don't truly belong to us, or they can be what uncles, grandmas, dads, mums, teachers, self-proclaimed gurus or others have told us we must be.

Read about personal metaphor again. Take some time to do the exercise that I recommended. If you've done it already, it's time to check and/or improve upon (if needed) what was done previously.

Guerrillas know the importance of metaphors, of dreams and of stories, as well they know the influence that these have on us. They also know how important it is to begin with the self.

Guerrillas believe that change is part of all things, inevitable—and somehow they want to be an active part in it.

Guerrillas devote themselves to what they do, so as to give the best of themselves, aware that the best for themselves is the best in this very moment.

A Guerrilla is curious and always finds a way to learn something new.

Guerrillas know how important their personal metaphors are and put all of themselves into making it emerge.

A Guerrilla knows that the right attitude allows impossible things to happen whilst the wrong one makes simple things harder, if not impossible period.

Remember—"Whether you think you can do it or you think you can't, you're right."

Starting out on the right foot means having the right state, putting all of yourself into something if it's really what you want.

Looking on the bright side of life is at times not about reaching the destination but about enjoying the journey.

It's never easy to make the first step, especially when the road seems a hard one.

A Guerrilla knows "if you want to go all around the world, start with the first step, then a second, then a third…"

Although Guerrillas are getting ready for success, as too are you now, they know that nothing can replace experience, and experience begins when we start to act.

I'm not asking you to believe unconditionally what I tell you.

Maintain a healthy disbelief, but don't let it become your limit.

So… how to do all this?

It's simple:

Start from "I can do it."

There are thousands of books on how important this is. Perhaps you haven't been told (or at least it may have been said by few) that if you don't feel this sentence to be yours with all of your body as you are saying it to yourself, little good will repeating it to yourself do, perhaps as you stand in front of the mirror. I suggest you open up your senses to your body as you say it and notice if the sensations that emerge are all in the same direction.

If you notice a harmonious movement of feelings, that's great. You're coherent or, another word to describe this harmony, congruent.

A Guerrilla knows how important it is to be congruent at the beginning of any new adventure.

If you feel something is wrong, it's better to stop before going further.

Starting with a bad feeling is like driving with the handbrake on!

Your body constantly sends you messages. If you find any incongruence, something must be done about it.

First of all, thank yourself for the message. Now you know you have to do something before starting out.

Your attitude, your congruence, will be crucial on this adventure.

Being your own ally is a great idea, in a partnership that leads to unexpected results and a remarkable quality of life.

So… how to resolve incongruence?

Let the feeling of incongruence guide you as you say I can do it. Think of something you could do that might reduce the incongruence and notice if the feeling decreases or even disappears.

For example, do you need any training to acquire essential new skills?

Or, do you need some further information to better enjoy your new adventure?

Or…something else perhaps?

Keep thinking and notice what happens to that feeling.

You are learning to give value to the signals from your body. You are starting a new kind of co-operation.

Keep doing this until you the sentence "I can do it" feels perfectly fine as it permeates your body.

For the same reasons, I insisted that your personal metaphor should give you a great feeling. I want you to move in desired directions with action plans that contain action in line with what you can do right now.

There's always room for improvement.

All right, so now "I can do it" is congruent with you.

Now practice what you are reading.

Practice, practice, practice, until these new choices become available, even at a very deep level.

At that point, and only then, check the results, judging them with healthy mistrust.

I once worked for an organization which had bought some new software intended to improve the quality and increase the speed of work. Many people had doubts and dismissed the software from the outset.

After six months, even the most skeptical colleagues had to admit that their working days had improved, both in terms of quality and in terms of time. All in all, things could be done in 20% faster than before.

Some who had believed in the software needed only three months to learn how to use it, while the non-believers didn't get results until six months after its inception.

The attitudes had been different. The first group had set aside any misgivings and had had a chance to assess the real effectiveness of the product.

In the end, the mistrust of the second group had worked against its members.

And in both cases, whether they'd liked it or not, everyone had had to use the new software by direct order of the management.

Here there's absolutely no order from on high. There's only one boss. That's you!

Make a commitment to yourself—your "order", if you like. Practice these new choices until they become a part of you.

I trust you!

At that point, they won't be suggestions, ideas or techniques—they'll be a part of you and you'll put them into action when needed.

In short, Guerrilla Time people:

Can do it!

Learn the method and the weapons

Practice, practice, practice

Check with healthy mistrust

2. Learning Guerrilla Time Competitive Advantage: the Human Factor

Doing as I've suggested, you've learned how to use the Guerrilla Time competitive advantage: *the human factor.*

You know how important metaphors are. You've created your own personal metaphor. You're sensitive to messages coming from your body and not solely from your mind.

(Pay close attention to language traps: mind and body are distinct purely from a linguistic perspective. In the real world there's no such boundary. In the real world we are both and neither, one being indistinguishable from the other. This is to bear in mind should the distinction lead us in unwanted directions rather than being of help to us.)

You've learned how to deal with your involuntary processes, proposing solutions to be validated by your feelings.

You've learned how important congruence is.

And, if you've carefully read this book so far, you've learned the importance of intention.

Now, when you set yourself a goal, besides checking your congruence, you should always ask yourself:

What's my intention behind the goal?

Remember the two people who came to me, having achieved their goals and…well…need I say, they weren't exactly thrilled.

Asking yourself this question at the very beginning will save you much suffering if any of the following are true: there are several possible goals capable of satisfying your intention; the goal that would be chosen without reflection only partially satisfies your intention; important parts of your life are potentially discordant with your goal.

Having discovered the intention (having made it emerge from within), you may find several ways to satisfy it and thereafter understand which is the best way for you. These will be goals which take your deepest needs into account and you will be much more congruent in pursuing them. Last but not least, the quality of your life will dramatically improve.

Investigating the intention behind goals (objectives) is mandatory.

It's also important to ask yourself what the consequences of pursuing your chosen objectives are.

You may acquire new perspectives, allowing you to enrich your objectives, to refine them and to make them more coherent with your deepest needs.

Learning about the human factor also means learning to choose your psycho-physical-emotional state.

As I've told you frequently, your psycho-physical-emotional state strongly influences your behaviors.

It influences the way you make your talents emerge, your knowledge and skills, the way you learn, your health, your whole life.

Let's take a look at a couple of ways to influence our state.

There are times when we need to recharge our batteries: for days of hard work when we need to be at our best; in the middle of a long drive when tiredness overwhelms us and we need to take a break; when we haven't slept well or whenever we need to be fresh, with full clarity of mind…

By practicing and practicing what's written in this book, you'll be able to enter a relaxed state easily, allowing you to recharge your batteries in just 15 minutes to a level normally requiring 2 hours of sleep.

Although this method has no side effects, it can't replace sleep!

Don't let the simplicity of the technique deceive you—it's very very effective. It's designed to favor deep relaxation and it really works. At a certain point the instructions may become difficult to follow. It's in that moment that you'll be able to give yourself over to relaxation.

Use this technique when you have enough time to do so. If you have something to do, set up an alarm, although on most occasions you'll be able to "wake up" at the desired time.

Sit (or lie) down in a comfortable position—at the beginning, as you learn this technique, a quiet place is strongly recommended—and notice the feelings from your body. Adjust your position until you feel completely at ease.

Aloud or in your head, start to describe your sensory experience, starting from what you see. Say what you see in 5 sentences.

For example: "I see a computer in front of me"; "to my left I see a blue wall…"

If you feel like closing your eyes, do so, then keep describing your inner experience (the light through your eyelids, images of trees or skies or rivers or mountains that flit into your consciousness).

Start from the outside experience. Then shift to the inner one when you feel you want to explore your internal world, doing so for the following steps as well.

Once you've made your five sentences describing your visual experience, make five from your auditory experience, either from external sounds or from internal ones.

Once you've made these five, make five more, inspired by what you are touching or by your inner feelings (kinesthetic).

After saying these last sentences, start again from the visual, this time with four.

Continue in the same way, with four auditory, then four tactile.

Then 3, 3 and 3…

At this point, you may already be relaxed. My advice then is to fully enjoy the experience. There's no need to go any further. You're already where you wanted to be.

If you're not quite there, continue…

2, 2 and 2…

1,1 and 1…

As you come back to the here and now, be aware of external tactile feelings, gradually shifting your attention away from what you sense inside onto the outside world. Enjoy your complete awareness.

Here's another choice for a high quality psycho-physical-emotional state.

What's your current posture?

How do you feel?

Our posture, the way we hold our body in space, has a deep and strong influence on the way we feel.

Let's see how to use it to our advantage.

Let's say we're walking to an important meeting.

Let's also say that we don't feel so good, despite having done a good job of preparation.

We could go there directly, and this is probably what we would have done before reading this book.

I suggest you test this out. When you're walking and not feeling good, notice how you walk.

How fast are you going?

How do you balance your body in space (leaning forward? to the side? rigidly upright?)

Are your jaw muscles tense?

Are you tense?

How are you breathing?

Start to change things. Let your mouth open up a little, loosening the muscles in your jaw.

How do you feel now?

Slow down a little. How now?

Modify your breathing, taking deep breaths from your abdomen.

How are things changing?

You'll notice increasing improvement in your state.

You were trapped in a cage that you'd built for yourself.

In our personal history, we create a strong bond between our psycho-physical-emotional states and our posture, our breathing, our movement, etc, such that, as we enter a certain state, our body automatically takes on that position and behaves like it's always done.

What I suggest now is that you use knowledge of these connections to your own advantage. Find a posture and a way of breathing which make you feel fine and keep walking this way until you sense a good state and thus know, after defining your intention, that it's time to have the meeting.

I invite you to be curious as to whichever method helps you increase the number of your choices in choosing your psycho-physical-emotional state.

The techniques I've just discussed are the result of years of research into personal and professional development.

3. Learning Guerrilla Time Weapons

You've learned how to develop a Guerrilla Time attitude, using the human factor to your own advantage. Now it's time to learn the weapons of Guerrilla Time, tools you can use to further improve the quality of your life.

There are more than 150 in total, all deployable without having to spend a penny!

All it takes is your time, energy, attention and your commitment to learning them and to putting them into practice.

Learning them means experiencing them; enough experience to make them your own, to make them part of you for the rest of your life.

In order to do this you need three things:

practice, practice, practice.

I'm interested in enriching and enhancing this book and the weapons arsenal of Guerrilla Time. If you have any weapons not mentioned here—something you use to make your time wonderful—please do contact me. There'll be plenty of room for your suggestions in the following editions.

Guerrillas know that time, energy, imagination and information are more important than money.

4. Action Plan

What to do once you've practiced and experienced all the weapons, turning them into truly available choices?

Choose which ones are most effective for you.

Bear in mind, you can only know which ones work best for you after experiencing them and turning them into choices. We human beings have a tendency to choose only what's most familiar, rather than what really works.

Remember my story about tennis…

Select the more effective weapons and put them into an action plan in which you specify which ones you want to use and how you want to use them.

You should also develop your Guerrilla Time Calendar. It will allow you to learn from experience, to discover which weapons are most useful, which ones have great potential realizable through practice and which ones are to be dropped for now, not having provided the expected added value.

Guerrilla Time is a process, a learning process, by which we attain a better quality of life.

5. Action, Action, Action

So, great, we're all prepared and now it's time to put our plan and our calendar into practice.

If the goal of the set-up phase is to be in the best shape to act, the goal of the action phase is to achieve the desired results and to learn from experience.

In order to do this, it's important to understand three basic aspects of the action phase:

1. The importance of intention: before stepping into action remember to define intention and objectives; remember, intention is like a lighthouse casting light upon your action.
2. The importance of your psycho-physical-emotional state as you act: your ability to see, listen and feel, the quality of your responses and your ability to change your behavior whenever it's ineffective with regard to your intentions. The selection of your behaviors depends entirely on your state; make sure, as you act, that you're in a state of excellence, the consequence of which will be great quality of experience.
3. We don't live forever. Guerrillas of Time know how important it is that they act to make the world better (at least a little) compared to the world they came into at birth. Acting this way is a gift that feeds our lives and the lives of others, while we live life and make it better.

If you think I've insisted a little too much on action, what will you think after reading each of the following words, without skipping a single one? (It's an imperative in case you wonder.)

Ready…(perhaps cross them off as you read them, just so you don't get lost in the action) …steady… act,

act, act and enjoy the action.

6. Monitoring and Feedback

We've planned, we've acted and we're acting, plus we want to learn from experience.

In this journey, ask yourself often: What's the intention behind what I'm doing? always double-checking if the answer is coherent with your chosen direction.

Our attention can become focused in less useful directions with respect to our needs. This question helps us re-establish our focus in such a moment.

Remember though, very useful things can come from less useful ones. Sometimes, when heading in one direction, we discover something that leads us somewhere else—Viagra for example…

Also remember that your life is not your destination. Life is your journey and the quality of your journey relates to the quality of your life.

On this journey, it can be extremely rewarding to look around with curiosity, even if this doesn't necessarily lead in the direction you've selected and settled on.

I've talked about balancing, and this is an example of it.

Getting back to our plan, regarding the roads we've taken, it's essential to monitor: their consequences, the pleasure we get from taking them and the satisfaction coming from that pleasure.

Have they led to results that you'd hoped for?

Have any useful undesired results emerged?

What other effective things could we have done?

Have we acted according to the feedback we received? How?

How, from the privileged perspective of external observers of what has happened during the day, can we feed tomorrow's actions?

As external observers, what feedback are we giving ourselves?

What have we particularly liked?

What can we improve and how?

As you witness what happens from the outside, watching yourself as the main character in a movie scene, as if you were your own expert consultant, focus your attention upon the quality of life of the "you" acting in the film.

That's what we're looking for.

Here we're interested in the quality of your life, which together we want to improve.

A Guerrilla knows the importance of planning.

A Guerrilla knows how it feels to have an unplanned adventure.

A Guerrilla knows the taste of action.

A Guerrilla knows how important it is to learn from other people.

A Guerrilla recognizes the magic power of self-given feedback to improve the quality of his/her life.

7. Improvements

Getting better!

You're not your current behavior. You are much, much more.

Whatever choices you've made in life so far, remember that they were your choices and that now they're your past.

A Guerrilla wants to learn from the past and to live in the present.

What do I long for?

What do I want?

Are basic questions. Essential questions.

Remember, many unhappy people ask for what they don't want, for what they aren't aiming at…

Think about it: their attention is bound to what they do not want and do not long for.

Don't go after what you don't want. Rather, start nourishing yourself with what you do want. With what you do long for.

You'll be working with your involuntary processes to move in the desired direction, namely, the one you *really* want to move in.

Some people, when they are told they can always improve, are overwhelmed with anxiety (some call it performance anxiety… what performance? I ask them).

To say we can always improve is to say we always have an opportunity.

After this sentence, stop reading for a while and notice how you feel. Notice your posture, your breathing, your muscles, the most tense and the most relaxed areas of your body. See if you can get more comfortable simply by changing your posture or your breathing. As you breathe in, imagine the air coming into your lungs as relaxing air and, as you breathe out, imagine the tension leaving your body as if you were breathing it out directly from the tense areas. Last but not least, notice that... you're alive.

Isn't it beautiful?

I remember being in hospital, stuck in bed, unable to move due to the malady I had at the time. When, after much (subjective) time, I could finally make it to the bathroom by myself again; when I could turn on the faucet and, with some difficulty, wash my hands with soap... magic! I caught myself crying, awash with joy from the sensations of rubbing my hands together, of the frothing soap, of the splash of water...

How many simple daily actions might deeply move us with their uniqueness if we fully experienced them?

You don't need to recover from a serious illness to do this.

And improvement is an option, never an obligation.

Knowing we can do things better gives us the energy to do just that.

And even if we don't improve in the intended way, we should love ourselves anyway.

Guerrillas love themselves. No matter if they haven't in the past, they've learned how to in the present.

Guerrillas know that the facts of life may not be easy to stomach; that some events really do challenge us. They also know that they "can do it" and even in their darkest hours that "the sun is always behind the clouds."

What can you do to make your life even better?

CHAPTER 6

150+ GUERRILLA TIME WEAPONS

ou're about to read about more than 150 solid tools for improving the quality of your life. Take your time as you do so

If you're tired, stop, have a break and rest.

If you feel that you've had enough stimulation for today, continue tomorrow.

The aim is NOT to finish reading this book as soon as possible: you're reading this text to make your life better.

To get the best for yourself out of these weapons you can adopt various strategies, which include:

1. run through them rapidly and then read them one at a time, practicing and practicing some more
2. read them one by one, putting the suggestions and ideas of each into practice and into action before moving on.
3. read them in small groups and then dedicate yourself to reflection, to practice and to action, one by one...

Suggestion:

Whatever be your choice and your preferences, I invite you, when you feel like deeply involving yourself in one of the weapons and getting the best from it, to read it and then to practice, practice, practice. And then at every re-reading of it you'll discover new opportunities.

A deep breath…

1. Time Is Life

The most important weapon to you, a Guerrilla of Time, is the awareness that time is your life. And to act accordingly.

If this idea really becomes yours, if you fully experience it, if you make it a part of yourself and act to live every single moment in its uniqueness, you begin to make your life better.

Refine your attention: be careful of what you say about time, careful of your perceptions of it, careful of how those who influence you see time, especially those who hold sway over you—do these words, perceptions, images help you make your time and your life better?

Or are they "inherited thoughts," things acquired from your culture, from the places you've lived, from books you've read, songs you've heard, movies you've seen, things that lead you to see your life as if it were happening to someone else, without your being an active part of it, without your living it in the way you want to live it?

Our way of thinking heavily influences our actions.

I want you to have more choices so as to become the protagonist of your time and of your life.

2. Time Is Subjective

Watching a clock, its arms moving at a steady universal pace, always the same, always the same, it strikes you that time might be something objective; that time is a thing which is "that way" and that way is the way time is. If such an idea becomes a part of you, well… you'll have far fewer choices as to how you live your life.

It would be as though there were nothing you could do about the evasiveness of time; tempus fugit, time runs away from us.

Whereas…

It's easy enough to see that time is subjective; that the way you experience time is entirely subjective.

Set a timer to count down from 30 seconds. Close your eyes and start your timer, then count from 1 to 30.

Did the timer buzz before or after you finished counting?

It all depends on the way we experience time. Time is subjective. It depends on you and your psycho-physical-emotional state. Repeat this exercise several times and you will have different results.

How does time pass as you're waiting in line at the supermarket and the cashier seems slower than a sloth with a hangover?

And how does it flow when you are having a ball and… it's time to do something else?

3. Ability to Alter Time Perception (Time Distortion)

Time is subjective and our perception of time varies according to our psycho-physical-emotional state.

If we learn to choose this state, can we alter our perception of time?

For instance, if we have something important to do and it seems there's not time enough, can we live that time as if it were more than enough, thus doing the thing easily?

Can we expand time with a special person and have a remarkable moment prolonged?

Can we feel the time spent in line pass in a flash?

Indeed we can. It may not be easy for most people, but it can be done.

This is the real time management: the ability to alter perception of time.

So… how do we do it?

First, learn as much as possible from the studies on it, starting with the fascinating hypnosis experiments conducted in the 20th Century.

Then there's your personal exploration of the matter, which can be very revealing.

What happens to you when time passes quickly?

What happens to you when it passes slowly?

These are different states and, as you well know by now, different states have different physical connotations.

How is your breathing different?

How is the way you hold your body different?

How is your muscular tension or relaxation different?

What happens if you choose the features of these physiological phenomena on purpose?

Enjoy your exploration!

Here's a suggestion: don't be distracted by anyone who tells you you're a weirdo or that you're trying to do impossible things.

We can distort time, it is possible, indeed it's only a matter of... time.

4. Conscious and Unconscious Processes

Our conscious capacities are severely limited.

An old but to this day valid piece of research affirms that our working memory is able to consciously manage seven plus or minus two (so between five and nine) items of information (George Miller, The Magic Number 7+/- 2).

At the same time, the unconscious mind is able to process more than two million data items.

What do you rely on when making up your mind or acting?

Although the data above cited remain a point of discussion, I'm interested in the underlying idea.

Western society has emphasized reason, our cognitive capacities, relegating our intuition and the power of our involuntary processes to a secondary role.

Although there exists no ontological separation between mind and body, voluntary and involuntary processes follow two very different logical channels.

"The logic of consciousness is incommensurable to the logic of the unconscious" wrote anthropologist Gregory Bateson.

To investigate the workings of those channels would be to go beyond the purposes of this book. However, discovering how to benefit from knowledge of this difference is essential: quality of life depends on it.

We've already outlined this, at times being insistent.

"Without the explicit involvement of involuntary processes, there is no lasting change." (John Grinder). That is "there is no lasting change in human beings unless involuntary processes are engaged."

When we talk about the human factor we mostly talk about the dynamics between voluntary and involuntary processes.

In books on traditional time management, content is 99% based on rational aspects. You may ask yourself (ironically at this point): How come these techniques don't work for me?

There is no change unless involuntary processes are involved.

How often do we try to change our habits and fail?

How often, when involved in a task, do we feel it's the wrong thing to be doing and hence results are poor?

How often do we fight ourselves, at the same time wanting a thing and not wanting it?

Knowing that we cannot solely rely on our rationality when choosing, when defining objectives, when performing actions, is an essential weapon for a Guerrilla of time.

A Guerrilla of time knows how important it is to constantly learn how to make the best of ourselves emerge, increasing the value of both voluntary and involuntary processes.

5. Congruence (Conscious and Unconscious Partnership)

Guerrillas of time know the value of congruence, when all of themselves are moving in the same direction.

There is an inner agreement, a partnership between voluntary and involuntary processes, which allows us to achieve remarkable and previously unimagined results, to tap into our most profound energies, to give value to intuition, to mind and heart. We act with complete awareness of our congruence, and we are congruent.

It is often said "those who are deeply convinced end up convincing"— strong congruence is sometimes called charisma, personal power or charm.

The power that congruent people have to influence themselves and others is immense.

We shape our future even when everything seems to be against us; in a stormy sea all our skills and abilities emerge to overcome difficulties and we sail safely to our destination.

A Guerrilla knows how congruence feels and looks for that feeling when it's not there.

Guerrillas constantly check their feelings, turning them into allies.

Guerrillas respond to messages coming from their bodies; messages which are also messengers.

Whenever there's a conflict, Guerrillas mediate, getting the best from their voluntary and involuntary processes.

Guerrillas take reason and feelings into account when it comes to making up their minds.

Guerrillas are led by their own feelings.

Guerrillas become extremely congruent when doing this. They know how important it is to make the world a better place, and act accordingly.

6. State

Guerrillas know that their psycho-physical-emotional states dramatically influence their behaviors and performance.

Guerrillas constantly seek to learn methods and techniques that allow them to acquire more choices with respect to their states.

Guerrillas know that if they want to change their behaviors to improve their results they have to act upon their states.

In short, Guerrillas:

- make up their minds only when in a good state;
- change their states if they are unsuitable;
- are sensitive to the feelings inside their bodies;
- know how to watch and to listen to others so as to understand the states of those they observe, knowing that these states influence these people's behaviors;
- make sure people's states are positive when talking to them. If they aren't, Guerrillas come back when they are or act in order to make them so;

- learn from experience whenever they don't achieve the expected results: Which state was I in when acting?

7. Direction

Guerrillas know how important it is to enlighten actions and so build their own lighthouses, establishing a direction in life.

They are very careful in defining this direction, because they know that our voluntary and involuntary processes, once it's established, move that way.

While defining direction, Guerrillas pay close attention to their own feelings: they want to be congruent, to establish a partnership with their involuntary processes.

While establishing direction, they make sure that they're in a good state. If not, they do something else first.

Guerrillas know the power of metaphors and stories to actively engage their involuntary processes.

Guerrillas know the importance of letting time pass; better to rest or to sleep on things so as to benefit from their involuntary processes.

Guerrillas know the power of images, sounds, feelings, tastes, smells and not only words—they know our primary representations are very powerful in defining direction.

Guerrillas know hitting upon direction is very important and they also know how important it is to keep their eyes and ears wide open. They may find something very interesting along the road.

Guerrillas follow a direction for as long as it's the desired one. If something changes, they take all the time they need to redefine the direction.

Guerrillas know that life is not about reaching a destination; it's the path they take to get there that matters. They know how to enjoy the journey, with all its possible adventures.

8. Areas of Life

When Guerrillas think about their own lives and the way they live their time, they know the importance of considering all areas of life.

Guerrillas don't focus solely on their jobs, businesses or any other singular thing… they consider themselves as a whole, in every area of life.

Guerrillas know that life is to be divided into areas. It is an artificial distinction which they create. Understanding human psychology, they are able to arrange their lives in different ways.

The classic distinction *work/family/friends/leisure time* may be an interesting distinction to monitor: How much time do I give to work? How much to my family?…

Is that time coherent with the direction I have defined in my life?

Or is there too much time for my hobbies or for…something else?

Understanding how we live our lives can be very important. It's like having a compass to guide us, letting us understand what we are doing on a daily basis and leading us in the right direction.

It may also be useful to divide our areas into sub-areas, proceeding to understand if time for each of the sub-areas is coherent with regard to our role, our objectives and the importance we give to that sub-area.

Yet it's not only quantity that's important. Quality too, is of the essence.

Remember to ask yourself such questions as: How much satisfaction do I get from my work? How much from my family?

And how much pleasure from these?

The same thing applies to sub-areas.

If we want to move in a certain direction, it's essential to consider different dimensions.

I advise you to consider how much energy you put into things and how much attention you commit to them.

The resulting map will have various "colors" and you will end up with a sort of "3D compass", which should clear things up a great deal.

As a matter of fact, the ultimate goal of a compass is to guide and orientate us.

If there's something wrong with the compass, it will lead us in the wrong direction.

Guerrillas know the importance of setting their own direction and also how important it is to have a well-made compass, a reliable tool in all weathers, independent of cloudy skies obscuring sun by day or stars by night.

This compass is a special one, which considers the human factor, and the Guerrilla him/herself.

Create yourself the different areas of your life, using a variety of classifications that satisfy you. Consider the factors important to you: painting a picture of the situation is very very useful. And may this picture of yours be full of color!

9. Intention/Objectives/Consequences

A Guerrilla knows the power of intention.

A Guerrilla knows the importance of consequences.

Many human beings find it difficult to think in terms of consequences, particularly the consequences of their own actions.

They may define an objective without investigating the consequences of reaching it. They may plan an action without thinking of its consequences.

Of course, it's not always possible to assess consequences before having an experience and then noting what follows. At times, however, it *is* possible, and also a very wise move.

Let's imagine the example of a drug being introduced onto the market. What would happen if consequences were left unchecked?

Take any law, the consequences of which were left unimagined.

Expected consequences of course may or may not come to bear; consequences entirely different from those expected may emerge.

It is essential that we keep our eyes wide open.

Asking ourselves "What might the consequences be?" is mandatory.

Answering this question allows us to better prepare ourselves for action, to refine or modify such action; even to think it better not to act at all.

To use the language of technology, our species, particularly some of its adherents, seems to have a sort of default bug.

The bug whereby the consequences of action are left unconsidered.

Mind you, I am talking about consequences, not effects. Effects are linked to causes.

As mentioned earlier, it is quite wrong to think in terms of cause and effect when human beings are involved: the dynamics of the situation are of a different kind. We can influence each other, even heavily, but we cannot "determine" someone else's actions, as in a cause-effect relationship.

Consequences, not effects.

Thinking in terms of consequences helps us become more responsible, the protagonists of our own lives.

Thinking in terms of consequences reminds us that we're living in a world where our actions generate changes and also reminds us that it's important to consider the impact that our initiatives have.

A Guerrilla knows how satisfying and rewarding it is to leave a better world and acts accordingly.

Guerrillas always remember the power of intention.

They also remember how essential it is to introduce intention when it comes to objectives, particularly life objectives, namely those we establish to make our life worth living.

When Guerrillas set an objective, they always ask themselves: What's the intention behind my objective? and then they act.

They let intention emerge from deep inside.

When it does, they find new ways to satisfy the intention, combining these ways to make them more effective. New objectives may emerge, and these may be even more effective in satisfying the intention.

If my objective is to become rich and my intention to be accepted by others, I'll soon discover that there are several ways to be accepted—money may be an option but it won't be the only one. Besides, it's not always the case that money leads to honest acceptance by others. What alternatives are there? How might I match becoming rich with other options and solutions that satisfy my intention to be accepted?

And only then will I do what all the other books say I should do: I'll specify my objective or objectives.

Enlightened by my intention.

Guerrillas know the importance of consequences.

Once the objectives that satisfy their intentions have been identified, they ask themselves:

What consequences might there be if I achieve my objectives?

Are these potential consequences aligned with my intention?

Remember that consequences may be evident in the short-term, medium-term and long term. Have you considered these various time-frames?

Intention and consequences apply well beyond objectives.

Guerrillas often ask themselves: What is my intention?

Doing so, they are checking that what they are doing is pointing them in the desired direction.

If Guerrillas want to improve their communication and do not get the expected results, they ask themselves:

What was my intention behind my behavior?

What were the consequences?

And once the intention has been identified, they find new ways to satisfy it. Then they check that consequences are aligned with intention.

If my behavior offends someone, when its intention was to compliment, I should find new ways of complementing until I can confirm that I've achieved the desired result, i.e. the person understands that we're dealing with a compliment!

When Guerrillas don't fully understand a person's behavior, they can ask that person:

"What's your intention?"

Understanding intention, both parties can find ways to satisfy it.

Whenever there's a conflict in progress, perhaps we should stop and clarify things... yep, you know... understand the intention of both sides; perhaps even the intention behind those intentions. At a certain point you may find that there's a common intention and it's from here that you can both set out to find a solution that satisfies everyone.

Very often in trade negotiations there's some provision or other which blocks negotiations and it seems impossible to find agreement. Well, just try asking: What's his/her/their/its intention in introducing such and such provision?

Often you'll find that there are several ways to satisfy the intentions of everyone present. Then, as if by miracle, you find the one which satisfies everyone.

We save time and relationships are of higher quality, as is life itself for all concerned.

I'd like to thank the creators of the intention and consequences model, John Grinder and Carmen Bostic St. Clair.

10. Overcome Alibis

"I haven't got time", "my job is different", "my situation is different", "one thing is theory, another thing is practice"...

Guerrilla Time has no time for those who hide behind alibis to avoid acting so as to improve their lives.

If you don't have time that's fine. You have an excellent reason to read and enact Guerrilla Time; time will emerge.

If you "can't find time to read it", choose a day of *read leave* rather than sick leave. Not just your time, but also your health will benefit from it.

Guerrilla Time is written around you. The human factor is at the center and takes into account not only differences but also your own differences, not only human needs but also your own needs, and your deepest ones at that.

I've told you from the very beginning: You have to act if you want a better life.

Any more alibis? If you want to keep on justifying yourself because this or that doesn't fit, because the situation is to blame, you'll always find alibis.

At this point, you'll also realize that it's your choice and you might find that you laugh at yourself; a great gift indeed.

I respect you and your choices, whatever they are.

There's a world of new possibilities and adventure at your fingertips.

11. Self-Evaluation

You've decided to give your life a twist, to make it better, and that's why you are reading *Guerrilla Time*.

How would you rate your time now?

It takes humbleness and realism and remember, it's you and only you that are assessing and evaluating the quality of your time.

Self-evaluation is a starting point.

How will you know that, after starting your Guerrilla of Time action, you are moving in the right direction?

How will you know your objectives are coming into being?

You need some tools that let you understand this. Self-evaluation comes from such tools.

Think about how you would give your time a score out of ten.

The criteria you would, the comparisons you would make.

All of this normally happens at an unconscious level.

Periodically evaluate the quality of your time and keep track of your improvements.

Remember getting better doesn't always mean improving. Learning is not a constantly ascending line, but rather features peaks and troughs. Overall though, the trend in learning is in the upward direction, as will be your satisfaction and your pleasure.

12. Satisfaction

How great is your satisfaction with your time right now?

Increasing satisfaction with your time is one of the objectives of Guerrilla Time.

Satisfaction is totally subjective. My goal is to increase your satisfaction (as long as it's yours too).

To begin with, I suggest you ask yourself from time to time:

To what extent am I satisfied with my time right now?

Then:

How can I increase my satisfaction with my time?

Leave the question hanging; think about it often and let solutions spontaneously emerge.

Focusing your attention is very very important. It's a catalyst for our voluntary and involuntary processes. It's an engine that works even when the ignition's off.

We want our attention to be directed towards our satisfaction.

Guerrillas are satisfied with their time and when they aren't, they step into action to make sure they are.

13. Pleasure

How can I increase the pleasure and enjoyment I get from my days?

Some say human beings seek out pleasure and avoid pain. Yet the facts of life seem to argue otherwise. Many people experience painful situations and do little or nothing to change the experience. Familiarity with their situations acts as a brake:

"I feel bad, but I know what to expect. In the end, it's not so bad."

If this describes your way of thinking, you can change your experience from one of familiar discomfort to one of new, exciting, perhaps unfamiliar, pleasure.

How can I increase the pleasure and enjoyment I get from my days? is an interesting question, which doesn't solve problems by itself, but which does set us in the right direction.

Some might say: What if I want to feel bad?

They should ask themselves: What's my intention in feeling so bad?

They could discover several ways to satisfy it without feeling bad. After all, we are talking about increasing the number of choices at hand.

Many people run away from pleasant things and from pleasure itself. They don't even want to feel it.

Why is that? some might ask.

My question is different:

How can we fully enjoy pleasure as a real choice, if the tendency is to run away from it? There aren't any magic solutions. You, however, already know of a simple, non-magical method. If you run from pleasure, the question is: What's your intention in running from pleasure?

Once again, let it emerge from deep within. Let some time pass, ask yourself:

"What's my intention in running from pleasure?"

And sleep on it.

Once the intention has emerged, look for other ways to satisfy it so that you can enjoy pleasure. It's a shame not to!

"How can I increase the pleasure and enjoyment I get from my days?"

May your discoveries be good ones.

14. Work Perception

Let's talk about work.

How do you feel when you say or think "I'm going to work"?

I know a great many people who feel bad in that moment.

If this happens to us, we have to be careful. This feeling is a message from deep inside.

Do you like your job?

In the modern era, there are millions who don't really choose *the* job, but rather do a job, thanks to which they get by, get to the end of the month.

If you find yourself in this situation, your job may well be a million miles away from the one you want and you do it because you haven't come across any alternatives. More often than not you experience your work in a bad way, and the consequences leave their mark…on your health, on the quality of a highly significant moment in your day, in the long run, on the quality of your relationships, including the one you have with yourself.

What to do?

Start from what you want, from what you long for, and never forget to aim for the sky… with both feet on the ground.

If what you are currently aiming for is not really what you want, remember to direct your attention towards what you actually want; remember to make an action plan, to act, to check feedback and to act again.

And as you do this, and you're doing the job you don't like, ask yourself: "How can I make this enjoyable?"

After all, it gets you to the end of the month.

Even in very difficult situations, there's always a way to find the positive side to things, with benefits for ourselves, for our psycho-physical-emotional state (which deeply influences our behaviors), for our health and for our well-being and quality of life.

How do you perceive your job?

How could you make your job more pleasant?

How could you make your job more enjoyable?

Do you know someone who loves the job you don't like?

How can this person like such a job?

Look, listen and talk to that person.

A long time ago, as a student, whenever I had to study a subject I did not particularly like, I studied it with those who loved it, I watched them, listened to them, spent time with them. And I liked the teachers who conveyed their passion for what they taught. I studied them carefully. I loved to hear them talk about their field of study, to see how their subjects excited them, to understand how they had developed such passion.

Mirror neurons, which tell us a lot about empathy, hadn't been discovered yet.

Looking back, I can see that empathy allowed me to like those subjects which I had not liked at the beginning. Learning became much easier and I could clearly see the results, first among which was my dealing with something that before I couldn't stand.

Then ask yourself: What do I really want?

If you're doing what you want, you are one of the few lucky ones (although luck does not amount to much without a personal contribution!). You are in a privileged position and yet you can still improve.

If you're not doing what you want to do, if you're doing what you don't want to do or if you feel that what you're doing doesn't belong to you, ask yourself this:

How could I act from now on (giving myself the time I need) so as to have *the* job and not just *a* job? Make a plan and act.

15. Role Description

Do you want to make your work time better?

Describe your role in a few words.

It often happens, both in organizations and at the entrepreneurial level, that a person's role is not that clear. If you are this person, you risk giving your time less value, you risk doing things your role does not require you to do whilst contemporarily forgetting about the things that are required of you. You end up doing something which would give the business added value and cause you less troubles if delegated to another.

Being fully aware of your role/s is extremely important if you want to make the best of your work time.

Now that you have described your role, pick a friend and ask him/her a favor.

He/she should listen to you as you describe your role out loud and ask you questions if what you are saying is not clear or makes no sense to him/her, up to the moment he/she fully understands your role and your responsibilities. Your friend should repeat the description back to you in his/her own words and answer your questions, if you have any.

So what's the advantage of this exercise?

It's pretty simple. The exercise tells you if your description was effective and it gives you the chance to clear your mind further.

A real friend (ideally who doesn't know what you do), who likes to listen and to help you out by doing you a favor (which you'll surely return), will allow you to have an external perspective, uninfluenced by the daily routine of your job, which often makes us take things for granted.

A new clarity of mind will emerge.

Doubts may also emerge, which you can clarify with yourself or your business.

Guerrillas understand how important it is to know their role(s) in their jobs, even if they are self-employed or the boss, so as to improve the quality of their work time.

16. Required Role

The required role is what an organization requires of its employees.

The way the organization communicates (or does not communicate) such a role is very strategic. Much wasted time, many disputes, misunderstandings between colleagues, all come from unclarified roles.

If you are an entrepreneur or a manager, remember to tell your partners and co-workers what their roles are and to make sure they've understood right. If they have, they will be able to better define their priorities regarding things to be done, they'll be better organized and they'll work better.

If you work for an organization which has not clearly specified your role, you can be proactive: Ask your boss to make it clear. It reveals your desire to be more efficient and it will have an impact on the quality of your job.

If you ever ask this thing, remember that the way present the request is extremely important. Find the most appropriate way, be in a good state, check your boss's state. State your intention. For instance: "I would like to be more efficient in my job and I'd love to ask some questions that might help me give the organization added value."

You and your organization will greatly benefit from that.

17. Acted Role

Your acted role is the one you put into practice based on your comprehension of the role itself.

What's the relationship between the acted role and the requested one?

Are you doing unrequested things, perhaps spending a lot of time and energy on them?

Or are you not doing things because you don't think they rest within the scope of your duties, and yet the organization expects them from you?

From these questions you can understand the importance of your acted role, which greatly depends on the "perceived role", namely, what you understand your role to be.

Ideally the required role matches the acted role and this in turn matches the expected role.

What is your acted role?

Does it match the required one?

How could you improve the relationship between required and acted role?

18. Expected Role

The expected role is the one other people, partners and colleagues expect you to perform.

It depends both on the way the organization explained each member's role and on each member's comprehension of it.

It also depends on the way you communicate your role. Remember, good communication makes others aware of your role and of what they should expect from you with regard to the organization's objectives and policies.

Perhaps it's happened to you that a colleague asked you to do something entirely different from what you usually do. And doing this thing cost you a lot of time, dare I say, wasted time.

Lack of adequate communication of one's role can lead to interpersonal conflicts. Some may think: "He doesn't want to do what I asked because he doesn't like me." Such a belief can trigger misunderstandings, which give rise to negative feelings in people and a great load of useless activity, consequently impacting on the organization's general climate.

How much time do we risk wasting this way?

How much of the organization's time is lost?

How much will the quality of work suffer?

19. Prescriptive and Discretionary Components

In every job role there are prescriptive elements, things which must be done, and discretionary elements, things which can be done.

It's very important to understand this distinction with regard to our role—and to the roles of our colleagues and our partners—so doing, we improve the quality of our work time.

Concerning mandatory things, we have some margin for interpretation—we can decide how to do the things we have to do, and that's where we'll act.

Regarding discretionary tasks, we have more choices; with these tasks more margin means greater responsibility. We need to prove that we "deserve" such discretionary power. Perhaps contrary to expectations, at every level of an organization, even at the top, there are discretionary and mandatory components to a job. Of course, for each role the interrelationship between the two types is likely to be different, but it's true that everyone has some degree of responsibility and with respect to this is to be held accountable for their decisions and for their results.

Guerrillas want to separate the mandatory from the discretionary in their minds. Whenever we want to act, it's important to understand where the limits stand and the boundaries lie.

Guerrillas want to improve their discretionary power, as long as this leads them in the desired direction.

A Guerrilla knows there are always ways to improve the situation.

20. Work Areas

Our intention is to improve the quality of our time. It may be useful to make a compass so that we understand how we use our time; an instrument to tell us if we're moving in the desired direction. When discussing areas of life, we outlined the importance of how we create such areas. Having created these areas, we can use them as a tool to verify that what we are doing is in alignment with our wishes and furthermore we can use them as a powerful focus for our future actions. The areas direct our attention, influencing our actions. This is why it's important to build multicolored maps of our lives, with the different categories and groups towards which we want to direct our attention.

As for the main areas, so for the sub-areas.

An area which is of particular importance and for which it is common to identify sub-areas is normally labeled "work".

Normally in that there are many Guerrillas of time who aren't too enthusiastic about calling their areas of profitable activity "work": they love what they do, they have a great time doing what they do and, in many cultures, when you love what you do and have a great time with it you are not working!

Guerrillas love their profitable activities and have fun whilst doing them.

In order to create sub-areas, two general methods exist:

Either you go top-down or you go bottom-up.

Starting from the bottom means listing all the tasks that make up your job. Once written down, the tasks should be read through carefully and we should think about how to organize them coherently, putting them together in a logical scheme.

Like this we build sub-areas from the bottom upwards, from single tasks.

The other strategy, top-down, asks that you think about the many ways your working activities might be divided.

It was according to this method that, as an entrepreneur, I understood how I was organizing my time; I understood how much time I put into every "area of activity".

I felt I could do much better. I had unpleasant feelings that led me to think about the way I was managing my work time.

In order to understand what was going on, why I had such feelings, I identified 6 working areas that I needed to monitor and then worked out how much time I used in each of these areas. The areas were:

- management of my company
- sales
- management of consultants and trainers
- training
- coaching
- administration.

First of all, I asked myself: How much time do I dedicate to each area at the moment? I then wrote down what I thought was the actual time given over to each one of them.

I then developed some acronyms for each area and, across a period of one month, I took notes of my activities (classifying them according to the identified areas) and of the time I spent on them.

At the end of the month I had a map, which read...

21. Time %

I thought administration had been taking about 10% of my time but...

The map was merciless—it was 34%. And there hadn't been anything special about the month; it'd been a normal run-of-the-mill month.

To my mind it had seemed that 10% of my time went to this area whereas the real figure was shockingly higher.

Such a figure was madness given my role, my capabilities, the added value wasted by all that time and all those tasks that could have easily been delegated to others; this was time and effort I could have invested in high added value activity, making the most of my abilities.

And I didn't even like administration anyway!

The numbers were merciless. I think, deep down, I had known they would be. And sure enough, once I had deployed the tools described in this book and I had changed the way I used my time, I started to feel quite different. All of that unpleasant feeling that had been living in my stomach was gone; I sensed a potent energy growing ever stronger the more I organized my time in keeping with the direction I desired to move in.

My feelings had come to me as a messenger and I had been able to interpret the message correctly and to act!

Keeping a compass can be demanding; nonetheless I advise you to do it… intelligently. Avoid being too precise (e.g. minutes, seconds) and read through the numbers calmly (they're only feedback and you've been wise to see for yourselves how you use your time). Create no more than 7 areas (better fewer if possible). We want our attention to be focused. If we focus it in too many different directions, our compass will become a giant distracter of attention.

Always remember your intention: to improve the quality of your life and, in this case, of your work.

How much time do you think you're dedicating to your identified areas?

Do you think it's coherent with your role?

When you have your data in front of you:

How much time do you actually give each single area?

Is it coherent with regard to your role and to the added value you can provide?

What improvements do you want to bring about in order to improve your job?

Every now and then, ask yourself if the classification is useful to the satisfaction of your intention. If is not useful enough, make it better.

22. Value

What's the value of every second you live?

Notice how you answer the question.

Do you answer in terms of its economic value?

If so, what else is *value* for you?

In my mind, giving value to one's time means living it as one wants; it means living as we wish to live.

How do you feel when you live as you wish to live?

When we live in this way, not only do we live better, but we can also give much more to the people around us.

"Emotions are contagious."

When you live with value, you live well; and when you have contact with others, this is conveyed. People look for you, are happy to be with you. Not only do you live *value*, you also give value.

What's the value of your time?

Once we've understood how much time we dedicate to our various activities, it is important to ask ourselves: What value does that time have? What value does that time have for me? And what value does that time have for the people I meet?

Does what you are doing have value for you?

23. Energy

Think of the times in which the things you do give you drive, make you feel full of energy.

How would you define the quality of your life in such moments?

WOW!

How often do you experience these feelings?

Would you like to experience them more often?

Think of those situations and notice what they all have in common, of the difference that makes the difference.

It's as if a part of you were so happy about the things you do that it fuels you with energy, even in moments when, under other circumstances, you wouldn't have this energy.

Enjoy these moments and learn from them.

Consider them in your time compass, give them value.

If you follow the suggestions in this book, you will find yourself experiencing them ever more frequently: we are learning to perceive the deepest of our needs.

Learn too from moments in which this doesn't occur, from things that seem to drain your energies rather than charge them.

When this happens, first of all, do something different!

The nature of your state deeply influences your behavior.

Then take note of which activities or situations these are, remembering that it's not the activities or situations themselves which "determine" the state, rather it's the way in which we face them.

And this can be changed. And you can change it.

In addition, you are getting great feedback from your body: what you are doing, the way in which you are doing it, at the moment makes you feel like this.

Write it into your time-compass, taking notes of the particular activities or situations. And if you want to improve the quality of your life, act: find new ways to test these activities, new ways to experience these situations; or, act by changing these activities, making of them others which recharge you.

We are talking about choices, and increasing the number of our choices gives us numerous opportunities to improve the quality of our lives.

24. Attention—Focus

Attention is one of the most limited resources we have. That's why where we focus it is of strategic importance for the quality of our lives.

Has this ever happened to you: You'd been on a wonderful journey and you'd had an extraordinary time; then you heard negative comments about the whole thing from others who had been traveling with you?

Sure, each one of us experiences things differently; there's wealth in variety.

But did you notice where these people brought their attention to bear?

While you were at the restaurant enjoying a special local dish, they, in the same restaurant, kept staring at the waitress, who was clearly not doing her job properly.

While you were enjoying a spectacular view from that same restaurant, they complained that "these chairs just won't stop creaking", and so on.

Where do you steer your attention?

Try this exercise.

Pick a person who you believe to be very different from you and for 15 minutes (ideally with the consent of this person) enter the "crazy world" of this person's primary experience; do exactly as he/she does, try to think exactly in the same way. Afterwards, feel free to laugh at the absurdity of the thing, but for those 15 minutes of exercise, commit yourself to it with total dedication.

After this experience, ask yourself: Where was my attention while I was this other person?

Would I have done the same things?

Would I have looked at the same things?

Would I have moved in the same way? etc…

No, in short. It's a different world.

And it's a different world in which your attention, while you were the other person, was steered in directions entirely different from those normal to you.

What an incredible learning experience!

Guerrillas know how important it is to direct their attention and are always learning new ways to do so for the greater enrichment of their lives.

25. Motivation

In this book I want to affirm something very important: Healthy motivation for you comes… from within you!

Who can be your own personal motivator if not you yourself?

Become your own personal motivator by beginning to develop a partnership inside yourself.

Learn to be sensitive to your body and the messages you receive from it.

Follow my advice and suggestions relating to congruence, to your personal metaphor, to state, to direction and… you'll discover that motivation flows from within.

You will wake up motivated, you'll act with motivation, you'll influence the people and the world around you with your motivation.

And if at times you don't feel motivated, this is special feedback that you've received. Seize upon it.

Maybe the time for thinking has arrived. Maybe new perspectives are ready to unfold… if only you shift your gaze…

Discover the pleasure of learning from your experience, discover the pleasure of healthy motivation… brought to life by you!

26. Proper Planning

Some people love to plan and so plan everything, down to the smallest detail. These people suffer terribly when the unexpected occurs—it wasn't part of the plan, and yet it happened! How is this possible?

There are people who love to live day-to-day, and so they never plan. For them the only thing that counts is what they are experiencing in the present moment. If they must plan, they are destabilized and have problems sticking to the plan, even a well-made one.

Guerrillas of time know how to enjoy every moment of life, how to taste its flavors, to appreciate its sounds and its colors. Guerrillas know how to plan and also how to plan time for the unexpected. They know, once having defined a direction, how to confirm that what they are doing is leading them in the desired direction. Guerrillas of time learn from experience and their planning constantly improves. Guerrillas know that not everything can be planned and let themselves be surprised by new happenings, seizing opportunities that arise from them.

Guerrillas know not everything can be kept "under control" and are happy about this: How many unexpected things might be the seeds of unimagined opportunities.

Guerrillas can choose to be completely in the here and now, enjoying the benefits of "timeless" time.

Guerrillas experiment and can appreciate the pros and cons of planning, getting the best out of it.

27. Habits

Human beings are creatures of habit.

Habits can be a mixture of blessing and bane. Often they are invisible prisons we've built around ourselves which inhibit our full living of live.

Guerrillas seek out their unproductive habits, those being the habits which lead them in an undesired direction. Guerrillas act to change their unproductive habits, aware that this may require time, practice and the ability to tolerate some healthy confusion.

When we explore new territory, this healthy confusion is a common companion. It's a sense of unfamiliarity which can hold us fast within its grip, causing us to abandon the new road for the old, even if the old is unproductive. Guerrillas are aware of this. They give themselves time to change, they commit themselves to practice and… they enjoy the benefits of knowing how to transform unproductive habits into effective and satisfying behavior for themselves.

Guerrillas consider their successful habits. They know that successful habits are often the most dangerous ones, in that they lead to the illusion that, if we keep doing what we've always done, we'll get what we've always gotten. They create the illusion that a certain habit is the sole road to success, transforming a world of choices into a cage of habits.

Guerrillas find new ways to be successful. They love to explore new paths so as to be more efficient and more effective and they enjoy exploring and exploring themselves.

28. Organization

Organize, organize, organize can be heard thundering out from all sides.

But with what intention? Guerrillas ask.

Guerrillas of time know organization responds to intention, their own intention.

And what is this intention? The aim of this book is to provide concrete tools to readers for improvement in the quality of their lives. Intention, the lighthouse, light itself, is precisely this: bettering the quality of life.

This intention being clearly stated, how can personal organization improve quality of life?

Ask yourself this question before going to sleep and then sleep on it. In the morning, see what emerges in response.

And then:

Organize… but how exactly?

First step: clarify a direction, making it emerge from within. We organize with regard to something. Organization as an end in itself leads nowhere. Example: What would have been the point of the maître d'aboard the Titanic continuing to organize the tables in preparation for the oncoming evening's dining once the ship had struck the iceberg?

Organization depends on intention, on the context in which we find ourselves.

Many of the tools you find among the weapons of Guerrilla Time might fall within the scope of this weapon's title (*organization*) despite my not mentioning them explicitly here.

And remember something very important: flexibility and adaptability are always needed.

29. Flexibility

In situations where little changes, planning can be easy, organization can be easy, forecasting can be relatively simple (or at least so it can appear).

On the other hand, when dealing with mutating scenarios…

Modern daily life is awash with sudden changes, high-speed mutations and rapidly-evolving contexts. Guerrillas of time know how important it is to organize with regard to the objectives they give themselves. They also know how to be flexible so as to effectively respond to challenges as they appear on the radar.

Flexibility as an end in itself, like organization as an end in itself, is of little use to those who want to live a life of quality. Both flexibility and organization depend on "where you want to go" for definition. Everything acquires color once we have direction, even when the sole purpose of that direction is to lead us, at our own choosing, into the full enjoyment of an adventurous experience.

And what if "I'm not flexible"?

It's not that we "are" or "are not" x, y or z, but rather that we behave in particular ways at the moment, ways that may be undesired or ineffective. We "are" much, much more than these behavioral modes; and we can learn how to activate new behaviors, can create for ourselves new choices and new opportunities.

"This is the way I am, flexibility is not a part of my character."

If you're happy with the situation and this is truly a choice for you, a choice I don't share in but do respect nonetheless, for me this is okay.

However, I will say this to you: You are worth much more, you can do much more… for yourself. You can have many more opportunities to fully live life, well beyond the cage in which you are living.

And then: What's your intention in answering this way?

Does it give you a feeling of self-assurance… or serenity of mind?

In how many other ways could you have self-assurance, peace of mind or the like, whilst developing new choices and new opportunities, whilst cultivating flexibility which allows you to achieve your objectives and to feel completely satisfied in the best way?

Guerrillas know that true self-assurance, that true peace of mind, as well as joy and satisfaction, come by processes, not by static means. "Everything becomes", and in this becoming, in this changing, we can have our say, we can do the things we like to do, for our own benefit and for that of others. Enthusiasm and joy are contagious! I'm not saying that all this can be had in a flash. I am saying: "You can do it!"

And with determination, patience, perseverance and the right tools the road goes from being a possibility for someone to being achievable for you, if you really want it to.

30. Exploration

Someone once said: "Life is a journey and the most important thing on this journey is not life's final destination but rather the quality of the journey, of this life's passage."

Observe a baby. Watch how he (or she) moves, how he watches, how he listens, how he smells and tastes things. Everything is new, everything is extraordinary, everything is amazing. Each experience becomes an opportunity to learn something new. Then if he's hungry, he finds a way to placate the hunger, if thirsty, a way to quench his thirst, if sleepy, he surrenders to slumber; and when his body needs to discharge its waste, he gives his immediate consent...

Every instant, every moment, unique.

Everything is experience. Everything is exploration.

If possible spend some time with some children up to the age of one and a half and do exactly what they do, without any judgment, analysis or rational thinking. Make sure the environment is safe and do exactly what they do. Become them for this time.

At the end of the experience, you will have re-opened the doors to something which was once familiar to you and which perhaps you haven't done for a long time.

In certain other moments it might become a useful choice for you.

Enjoy your exploration.

31. Balance

A Guerrilla of time lives in the realm of "I can" and not in the realm of "I must".

All the things we're looking at together, all the tools we're discussing, they're all possibilities.

The same is true of balance.

Some say: "We must be balanced."

They are trying to make universal something which they personally think is right and fair.

What they say to themselves has a certain sense to it. But for those who listen, it has a certain *other* sense, i.e. the listener's sense.

The question is: balance how specifically?

Guerrillas of time know their point of reference is themselves and they know, given that they are in touch with their own bodies, when it's the right moment to balance something and also how to balance it.

How to balance personal life and work life, for example.

How to balance time dedicated to our families with that dedicated to our friends or with that dedicated to work or to colleagues.

There is no single way of balancing any of these things. There are as many ways as there are human beings.

With this book, I hope to have offered you the means to understand which ways are best for you.

With these tools, questions, ideas, suggestions and metaphors you can become a unique, self-customized, Guerrilla of time.

32. Action Plan

Over 90% of people who read a given book or attend a particular training course don't act upon the information, ideas or tools presented to them in the process.

Well, if you are one of these people, stop reading and throw yourself into something else that gives you greater satisfaction, greater reward or greater quality.

I don't want you to merely read this book, be delighted by it and talk about it enthusiastically with your friends. I want this book to become experience for you and, for this to happen, you should practice and practice and practice some more. And, to give greater value to this practice, what can you do?

Quite simply: Make an action plan.

An action plan helps you draw the maximum benefit from this book. As it helps you draw the maximum benefit from any situation requiring action.

An action plan need not be perfect. Attempts to render it such may mean you never finish it and consequently a lack of action. An action plan is a guide and is important in that it focuses our attention.

An action plan is to be improved through action and action's feedback.

A well-made action plan can be your greatest ally.

Write into your action plan which Guerrilla Time weapons you want to activate, your intention in activating them, when you will activate them and for how long they will remain active. All you need is a four column piece of paper, or a word processor:

Your four main titles should be *Weapon, Intention, When and How Long*.

You can add further columns under titles which represent important factors for you personally.

Act now. Make your action plan for the weapons covered so far.

33. Effectiveness and Efficiency

There are many results-oriented people who don't consider how they achieve their results. They don't consider the resources committed to achieving them and they often neglect the factors of time and quality of time. Such people are effectiveness-oriented, not efficiency-oriented.

Other people want to do things right; they're efficient, but not results-focused. They aren't effective.

A Guerrilla of time understands the importance of results and also the importance of the road leading to those results.

Guerrillas of time know how to combine effectiveness and efficiency. They always think of the two things together, never forgetting that both are important.

34. Action, Action, Action

Do you know the biggest difference between those who achieve results and those who don't?

Luck, you say.

Nope. The world is full of lucky people who don't achieve their desired results; these people don't know how to seize opportunities as they present themselves.

Talent, then.

Nope. The world is full of talented people who live very poor lives, far from their desires.

Perhaps it's money.

It's not money. The world is full of rich and unsatisfied people who do not achieve their desired results.

Every one of the above can factor as an important ingredient in the results recipe, but what really makes the difference is …action!

Act, act and…act again.

35. Feedback, feedback, feedback

Action is fundamental. Having all our senses fully switched on as we act is equally fundamental: We have to *nourish* ourselves with the feedback from our actions

And according to our objectives, with flexibility, we should change our behavior if it's not effective.

Simple, isn't it?

Hardly.

This use of feedback appears simple on the page, but in practice requires we constantly develop and improve our skills, throughout our lives, in the here and now.

A Guerrilla of time knows how important it is to live in the here and now, and to live in it actively so as to achieve results. We can't keep our eyes wide open and our ears pricked if we dally too often in pasts or in our possible futures. The ability to remain in the here and now is essential (just like the ability to "project" oneself into the future is essential when it comes to planning).

Guerrillas of time know how important it is to be flexible with their behavior. Like this, if they see something is leading them in an undesired direction, they can change direction.

An airplane takes off with a destination and follows a route for the flight. But if the flight instruments or information from the ground signal danger, perhaps a change in weather conditions, pilots can change route so as to arrive at their destination.

A Guerrilla understands how to make feedback bear fruit. They understand how to respond to it effectively.

A Guerrilla understands the importance of intention and objectives, the things which give meaning to feedback.

36. Giving yourself feedback

Giving ourselves feedback can be an effective way to learn from experience.

Giving oneself feedback doesn't mean doing what is for many a preferred sport, namely, ferocious self-criticism. Those who practice this sport experience a reduced sense of self-effectiveness and, instead of learning positively from negative experiences, they tend to repeat negative experiences.

Giving ourselves feedback doesn't mean we endlessly lambaste ourselves about something we've done, reliving the experience to the nth degree, way beyond its original incarnation.

If your desire is to truly learn from experience, giving yourself feedback and not being a victim of it, here's something you should know…

Reliving an experience from long ago, with all of our senses tuned towards it as if it were happening in the present, strikes us inside with similar force to that which we would feel if we were experiencing the thing again for real. And with this repetition of the experience, the experience is concretized inside us, becoming a model for future actions but not necessarily in the positive sense of learning from it. Instead it becomes an automatic response and we repeat rather than learn.

So how should we learn from "mistakes"?

A method that helps us to this end is known as "personal edit" (developed by John Grinder).

This method has two prerequisites. The first is that we have the choice to see and listen to an old experience as if we were watching a film. A film in which we play the lead, but in which we are not "contaminated" by the emotions of the past moment. I'll give you an example using myself as the subject; when I use the name *Andrea*, I'll be talking about the images and sounds of myself that I project into the movie context. So, I can see Andrea in front of me. He's very tense because he's in a meeting which isn't going well. He's not getting the results he expected. Here I am, the coach, in a great state, relaxed as I watch and listen to Andrea. Doing so, I'm able to put together some useful advice which I'll give him when he's finished. Watching Andrea from this position of coach, from the outside, is a strange experience. How strange his voice sounds to my ears. I think it's safe to say that all of us experience something similar the first time we see or hear ourselves from an external perspective, perhaps when we hear a recording of our voices or when we see ourselves in a video recording.

Some manage to do this exercise rather easily, whilst for others a little practice will be needed. An useful tool is a camcorder combined with a patient friend to operate it. Acting out the experience for real, then watching and listening back to yourself can really help develop this skill.

The second prerequisite is the ability to relive situations as if they were occurring in the present moment. Practice with situations in which you felt good or very good. Note if you are able to relive them as if they were happening in the present moment.

At this point, having confirmed your ability to stand in what are respectively known as the third position (that of the coach) and the first historical position (you, reliving a situation) "personal edit" becomes easy.

Put yourself in the coach's position, look and listen to what happened during the period of time in question (for instance, your most recent working day). Do that and nothing else. Then pick out, still from the coach's position, what you particularly liked. I know it can be difficult to see the good in certain situations, but do try your best to see the positive elements.

Then, as coach, identify those things you would like to improve and "cut" the unwanted "clips of film". Replace each of these cut clips with three different alternative scenes which show you acting as you would prefer to see you act.

Watch and listen back, still in the coach's position, to the "edited" movie and, if satisfied (everything is now truly wanted and desired), only then, relive it in the first position (with the various alternatives you've introduced).

Turn this into a habit and let the results surprise you.

37. Monitoring

We've created our wonderful action plan, we're acting, we're being nourished by our feedback and we're adjusting our route where necessary to get safely to our destination.

Now what?

Stay alert: opportunities can emerge, difficulties can arise, changes can become necessary.

It's essential that we monitor both our path and our plan.

It's not always easy to keep our eyes and ears wide open.

Nowadays the flow of information is so intense that we are literally bombarded by it.

We need a light to guide us, our intention. We need tools for monitoring, to help us with the task, to help us tell what's relevant from what's not.

Monitoring requires organization. Organization of the means, tools and resources at our disposal.

Monitoring requires that we have access to the psycho-physical-emotional states which enable us to monitor.

Airport staff who have to make sure that people aren't carrying dangerous items know something about this. Concentration, the ability to rapidly regain a lost state, the ability to keep one's senses fully switched on, are all required.

In today's world there are numerous and varied signals which can slip under the radar of our attention, signals which may indicate an opportunity, or danger, or new ways to better achieve what we truly want.

These signals are impossible to pick up without our own personal system of monitoring.

A Guerrilla knows the importance of monitoring and makes intelligent use of it.

Guerrillas continue to learn how to recognize "the signals" which can improve their quality of life.

38. Learning from Ineffectiveness

Some time ago I met a very old lady. That day she was particularly talkative. Outside there was a tangible air of spring. As her eyes waltzed across a horizon holding up a stunningly bright blue sky, she said to me,

"You know, Andrea, one thing I've learned in my life is that every day, *every* day, you can learn something new."

We can always learn.

We can learn from our excellence. We can also learn from things that turned out to be ineffective.

Today more than ever, correctly predicting the consequences of an action can be a very complicated endeavor. And if we don't act, period, in most cases, predictions cannot be made, period.

In today's world, achieving results different from those expected (which some might call mistakes) is not difficult at all.

The only way to avoid this state of affairs is to not act at all and so condemn yourself to a spectator's life, chained to your armchair.

Those who act know that results may be different from those expected or hoped for. At times they can be even better than those we had hoped for, at others they show that the path we've trodden up until now was ineffective.

A Guerrilla of time knows how to learn from experience and treasures experiences of ineffective action, learning from them new ways to achieve desired results.

Guerrillas of time don't cry over spilt milk. They nourish themselves with solutions rather than with problems.

Guerrillas of time know that the big danger comes when they stop. So they keep on acting, keep on learning from feedback.

Guerrillas of time know how to laugh at themselves while thinking of their "mistakes". They're able to ask themselves: "How else can I satisfy my intention to achieve my desired results?"

39. Learning from Within

Learn, learn and learn some more. The world gives us endless opportunities to learn new things that have the power to make our lives even better.

A Guerrilla knows learning is fundamental.

A Guerrilla also knows learning from within is crucial.

What do you like?

What makes you happy?

What makes you feel good?

What don't you like?

What do you love to do?

How do you love to do it?

Continue to ask yourself questions and to notice how you live your experiences… inside.

You'll learn things about yourself that you wouldn't even image.

40. Celebrate

When you achieve what you consider to be remarkable results, remember to celebrate.

Sometimes, if you haven't celebrated for a long time, you should ask yourself:

Am I not too hard on myself? Which criteria do I use to measure my satisfaction with my results?

It's a good idea to reward yourself for your achievements. But bear in mind that life is more than just results. Life is the path that leads to them.

Every now and then, just celebrate for the sake of it, acknowledging that being here and being alive are already great results.

Have fun!

41. 80-20 (the Pareto Principle)

20% of our time is responsible for 80% of our results.

This principle, known as the Pareto Principle, reminds us that we can always get better.

Try to understand what that strategic 20% consists of for you. Then ask yourself how to better use the enormous slice of time, the 80%, that's not used as effectively as it could be.

What could you do to improve the quality of all that time?

How could you get greater satisfaction from it?

How could it be better aligned with the direction you've chosen to follow, with your intentions and with your objectives?

Guerrillas of time know that there's always room for improvement and that we can discover ever more satisfying ways to live our lives.

42. Priorities

Defining priorities is very important if we want to know where to focus our attention.

Sometimes we become lost on the mountain of things to do. We do things because they're on the list of things to do. But did we make sure they were ranked well in terms of priority?

Priorities derive directly from our personal metaphor, from our chosen direction, from our intentions and from our objectives.

If we work within an organization, our priorities will depend upon our role.

Many are those people who move constantly, often at great speed, and, like mad sparklers, fizz and spit enthusiastically, but in the end accomplish little.

It's you that chose your direction, you that desire to satisfy your intentions and you that have chosen your objectives. Remember to put things to do in order of priority.

Make sure, day after day, that you fulfill your top-three strategic priorities.

And, at the end of the week, you'll notice how many important things (for you) you've done.

43. State-priorities

Before sorting out your priorities, always check your state.

How do you feel?

Your state influences your performance and, when dealing with priorities, it's a priority that you're in an excellent state!

44. Conscious and Unconscious Preferences

One of the most interesting things to discover about ourselves is that we have rational preferences, of which we are aware, and preferences in our unconscious minds, of which we are not.

When preferences of which we are aware (conscious preferences) and those of which we are not aware (unconscious preferences) are aligned and heading in the same direction, we feel a sense of congruence and coherence inside; all our energies are heading in the same direction. When this happens our chances of success increase tremendously, as does our satisfaction.

When conscious and unconscious preferences are not aligned, we're like a car with the hand-brake on: We churn out heaps of energy and crawl forward at a snail's pace.

Many of the exercises in this book aim to develop sensitivity to unconscious preferences and to build a partnership between voluntary and involuntary processes.

Enjoy your exploration.

45. Unconscious Check

The development of body sensitivity is fundamental if we want to live a life of quality and if we want to perceive our unconscious preferences.

Imagine you have a plate of food in front of you and you believe that you want to eat it. You can check if this is true by entering a state of body awareness. Look at the food again… see how you feel?

At times you'll find that it's exactly what you want to eat in that moment. At others that it was in fact a rational desire, a whim of the mind; the body perception check reveals that the desire didn't come from your body; that you weren't really hungry, for example.

Being sensitive with regard to our bodies and with regard to preferences revealed via unconscious checks allows us to live life in ways which are highly coherent with our individual selves, with a more complete understanding of ourselves and also of those around us.

Congruence/incongruence is a universal of the human species. With the ability to observe it in others, you'll discover when people are being congruent and when they are not (what they're saying in words is not what they're saying with their bodies). Incongruence may be a conscious choice, although it often slips past the radar of consciousness undetected.

Guerrillas of time are very sensitive to congruence and incongruence in themselves and in others.

46. Internal Negotiation

What should we do when there is dissent between our conscious and unconscious preferences over what to do? When there's dissent over a decision to be made?

As when two friends find themselves in disagreement, the best solution is usually found through negotiation and the admission that "We're in the same boat here."

The solution which emerges may be far better than any proposed individually by either friend. Or perhaps one of the two friends comes to understand that the other's position makes more sense and is more effective in light of the common desired direction.

Remain in contact with your body. If you notice unpleasant sensations while thinking on a decision to be made, these sensations can be your allies. Think of a variety of ways to make the decision and be sensitive to what your body tells you. During this interactive process, you'll discover how new options often emerge spontaneously, options which completely satisfy you and allow you to feel good about the situation.

Guerrillas of time are acutely aware of the importance of congruency both for the achievement of desired results and for a life experience of superior quality.

47. Metaphors

Metaphors are extraordinary creatures. Their influence on all human beings runs deep.

Which metaphors can be found deep down inside you?

Which cartoon characters influenced you the most?

Which songs?

Which fairy tales?

Which stories?

Which novels?

Which movies?

Which of these metaphors are you currently living?

Are they metaphors that help you move in the desired direction?

Which will you keep?

Which will you modify?

How?

Take your time. Let these questions (one at a time) cause answers to emerge.

48. Left Brain-Right Brain Functions

The following is a basic list of functions usually attributed to either the left or the right hemisphere of the brain.

Left-brain functions:

- analytical thought;
- logic (cause and effect);
- detail oriented;
- words and language;
- knowledge of object names;
- sequential processing;
- divides the world into identifiable, nameable small pieces.

Right-brain functions:

- holistic/systemic thought;
- intuition;
- creativity;
- big picture oriented;
- symbols and images;
- knows the functions of objects;
- simultaneous processing;
- connects the world into related wholes.

Which hemisphere do you think you use the most?

Design activities for yourself aimed at developing the hemisphere you feel you use less.

Guerrillas of time are able to use all of themselves and all of their brains in the living of a life of quality.

49. Tasks

Once your priorities are defined and ordered according to importance, it's useful to have an action plan featuring specific tasks to complete so that you are moving in the right direction.

These specific tasks can be put onto to-do lists, ordered according to priority and to a calendar. When carrying out the tasks it's very important to always remember the intention behind the task; for those of us who have the habit of setting ourselves many tasks, there's the risk that the compass gets lost, that we become trapped in the details. We risk missing the big picture, the vision of the whole which allows us to correct our route where necessary.

50. State-tasks

Before writing your list of tasks, remember to double-check your state. Is it an appropriate state?

If the answer is yes, write your list of tasks. Remember that the tasks are important, so it's essential to act, to carry them out.

51. Check list

Creating a check-list can be useful for many situations. Create a bullet-pointed list, checking off points as you move down the list, ensuring that the important things get done.

How could you use check lists to improve the quality of your life?

52. Organizational Processes

It must be stressed how important organizational processes are in organizations, despite this book's not being directly addressed to organizations. Of course direct consequences for organizations do derive from the application of this book's content, namely increases in productivity and in personal and professional satisfaction.

A careful analysis of organizational processes often asks the following questions:

What's the intention behind this organizational process?

Will the process' application satisfy the intention?

Will there be any negative consequences deriving from the application of this process?

Do efficient and effective alternatives exist which can satisfy the intention behind this process?

Infinite quantities of time, infinite quantities of energy and heaps of commitment are literally thrown away by people in organizations precisely because these questions are not explored with the due attention and frequency.

Guerrillas of time know how much organizational processes impact on the quality of their time. They are proactive (when it's intelligent to be so) in urging, proposing and finding new and more efficient and effective solutions for the betterment of the organizations for which they work.

53. Responsibilities

Regarding work, one important aspect to be clarified is one's responsibilities.

What are these responsibilities?

Responsibilities normally arise from one's role and therefore organizations, in order to give value to their collaborators' time, should define it clearly and comprehensively.

If you are an entrepreneur or a professional, it's fundamental that you clarify your role with regard to yourself.

Within your areas of responsibility, what possible choices do you have and what constraints?

Ask questions, ask questions and ask questions again are three great pieces of advice.

Questions that are simple in appearance allow for clarifications which open the doors to new degrees of efficiency and effectiveness.

What are the criteria for assessing my conduct?

How do I monitor my performance?

What else should I know so as to meet my responsibilities effectively?

These questions are not only linked to the quality of life at work and to efficiency and effectiveness on the job. They also have a direct link to quality of life itself.

54. Importance – Urgency

Too often nowadays, lives are led in response to urgency, with things being done according to their urgency. And in a world where everything is urgent, stress levels have increased to such heights that, very often, things crucial to us personally, or to the organizations for which we work, don't get done.

A very simple tool to correct this trend is the so-called *Eisenhower Matrix*.

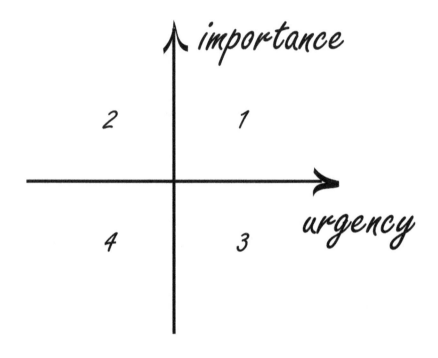

importance_urgency

In the above diagram, we can see how the Eisenhower Matrix—or if you prefer the importance/urgency matrix—considers two parameters contemporarily: importance and urgency.

Placed next to the driver of modern activity—urgency—is the other fundamental element to consider when deciding how to act—importance.

While urgency can be seen as time remaining to complete a task or activity, importance has to do with our intentions, our direction, our objectives and, when speaking about companies and other organizations, our role as well.

A thing is important to us according to parameters set by us or by the organizations for which we work.

Looking at the diagram, we can see four distinct areas (quadrants).

Quadrant 1. Urgent and important activities:
These are things to be done immediately, to be placed in order of priority straight away and dealt with as soon as possible; the fuller this quadrant, the more we tend to feel under pressure (after all, speed and precision are of the essence here); organizing oneself so as to reduce the number of activities in this quadrant is a very intelligent choice;

Quadrant 2. Important and non-urgent activities:
These are things to be done which carry the highest risk of procrastination; given that they aren't urgent, there's the risk that they get postponed, until… they become urgent… leading to saturation of the first quadrant and massive doses of stress. So what to do? Plan these activities into an agenda and do them before they become urgent (a great way to reduce overcrowding in the first quadrant).

Quadrant 3. Unimportant and non-urgent activities:
It's worth assessing whether things in quadrant 3 can be delegated to others for whom those things are important in light of their roles. If these tasks cannot be delegated to others, they should be dealt with in non-strategic moments of the day.

Quadrant 4. Unimportant and non-urgent activities:
Unimportant and non-urgent activities are activities to be reconsidered at a later time; in other words at a future date we should check whether they have become more important or at all urgent.

For many, the Eisenhower matrix is an essential tool for planning things in order of priority. This simple diagram helps them to made rapid decisions, simultaneously taking into account the parameter of importance and that of urgency. Use this tool and notice how it can improve the quality of your personal organization and, therefore, the quality of your time.

55. Efficiency Curve — Productivity Curve

One of the most important features among Guerrillas of time is their relentless pursuit of a better understanding of themselves.

When do you feel that you're giving the best of yourself?

When, on the other hand, do you feel you're not firing on all cylinders?

And when do you need a break so as to recharge your batteries and set off again with a bang?

Being able to assess how you feel and to adjust what you are doing in line with these ways of feeling can hold considerable surprises when it comes to improving the quality of your time.

It may be that early in the morning we run on a low burn and only later on in the morning do our engines spin up to full potential.

When shall we concentrate our most important activities?

Precisely, when our efficiency curve is high i.e. late morning.

In the early morning ignition phase, then following our peak efficiency, when there may well be need of a cool down, we'll engage in less strategic activities, perhaps ones that are more repetitive and familiar.

Guerrillas of time know how to manage commitments and activities according to how they feel. Guerrillas of time know how to change the way they feel when facing activities that are important.

56. Meeting Management

Meetings may be excruciating for organizations and they may be delightful. Just consider that the number 1 cause of wasted time in organizations is badly managed meetings.

Immeasurable sums of money are thrown away, enormous amounts of energy wasted, in meetings improperly convened and managed.

Well managed meetings can turn into an extraordinary competitive advantage.

It's understandable from the above that, on meetings, there's a lot to be written.

Here are some suggestions essential for improved meetings.

Before the meeting
- is the meeting the most suitable instrument for the satisfaction of the proposed intention/s? (assess alternative tools and procedures)
- hold meetings only when necessary
- write an agenda containing objectives and the criteria to understand if these have been reached or not, starting from the quick and easy to the long and difficult
- clearly schedule the beginning and the end of the meeting
- assess the investment of the meeting (economic value, "social" value)

Opening the meeting
- confirm the time available for the meeting
- clarify objectives and list points for discussion
- establish a clear method, accepted by all, to avoid inappropriate digressions and to move the meeting along according to the provisioned topics

During the meeting
- at the end of each topic: who does—what—with whom—by when
- ask: What's the intention?
- end the meeting at the scheduled time with a clear follow-up plan for after the meeting

Make of your meetings your delight!

57. Effectiveness in Public Speaking

Speaking in front of an audience seems to be one of the greatest fears among human beings.

At the same time, public speaking is of fundamental importance in various moments of our lives: in meetings, during conferences and seminars, among family, during celebrations…

Effective public speaking requires knowledge.

Effective public speaking requires competencies.

Guerrillas of time know how important it is for the quality of their lives to learn effective public speaking.

Guerrillas of time always find new ways to learn how to better themselves for communication in public.

58. Managing "Difficulty and Procrastination"

Many people postpone activities which they see as difficult.

If you're among them, try this strategy.

Start the day with activities which require little time for completion (approximately no more than 10 minutes each) and which you see as easy. Do three of four of these (for a total of, let's say, 30 or 40 minutes) and you'll immediately feel in tip-top condition.

After experiencing the satisfaction of "getting things done", immediately start, with this feeling and enthusiasm, the first difficult activity. Give yourself the right time to do it and do it. You will often find this activity much easier than expected. Once completed, reward yourself for the achievement.

Now you can get on with other things or start another supposedly-difficult task, if you're feeling enthusiastic and capable of overcoming the challenge.

Have you done that too? Congratulations, reward yourself again!

Then get on with other activities, perhaps easier and more gratifying ones.

Setting yourself the goal of performing one or two difficult tasks by the end of the morning, and building success after success, you will pass from procrastination to an appetite for a challenge, and you'll act.

This method is just one of the many that come from understanding the human factor, and above all from "knowing thyself".

Increasing your sensitivity towards yourself, discovering how you act best, you'll realize that there aren't absolutely easy or difficult activities. It all depends on the psycho-physical-emotional state that you are in as you carry out the activities.

Turn what has always been a limit in a strong point.

Learn to nurture your sense of self-effectiveness, your capacity to do things and the appetite for doing them. And you'll discover that you do them well.

If you think you won't be able to do something, set yourself the goal of doing your best, with no expectations of whether you'll be able to or not.

If you have anxiety about perfect performance, prescribe yourself at least two "mistakes" in the execution of the thing.

Guerrillas of time always evaluate various opportunities, noting which might work well for them and then making use of them. Guerrillas know that certain strategies may not work in certain moments, while in others they may reveal themselves to be the best possible solution.

59. Stress? No, Thanks!

Here comes an uncomfortable truth.

Stress doesn't exist. It's only a word.

Stress is not an entity, something concrete. It's what we decide to do in response to what happens to us, externally or internally.

The bad news is that stress has become such a widespread phenomenon as to contribute in a decisive way to the expedition of all kinds of diseases, poor performance, dissatisfaction…etc…

The good news is that, with the right tools and with your disciplined practice, you can learn to avert it.

And should you ever feel stressed, you can learn to rid yourself of it.

The word stress, in the common sense of its meaning, has a negative connotation and is used to describe what is technically called distress, or negative stress.

There is actually another type of stress, known as eustress, which allows us to reach new objectives, to be motivated and to be full of energy so to overcome obstacles we previously thought insurmountable.

60. Averting Stress

In order to effectively avert stress, the first thing to do is to "know thyself".

Stress is a physical response that occurs when facing external or internal events.

Our ability to perceive our bodies and to notice how we physically respond to events is an extraordinary tool which allows us to avert stress.

Indeed, being sensitive to our physical responses (muscle contractions, irregular breathing, etc.) we can identify the circumstances which, at this time in our lives, provoke said physical responses, which in turn lead to what is known as stress.

Let's learn to recognize these responses and let's learn to act upon them.

If, for example, we notice excessive contraction of our shoulder muscles, let's learn through exercise and effective breathing how to relax them until our physical response to that situation is one that allows us to face that situation, without unproductive responses being generated by our bodies.

Another useful tool may be that of learning relaxation techniques and when we notice, for example, that we are responding with excessive contraction we can carve a few minutes out for ourselves to relax and to recover proper use of our bodies.

There are many occasions for this.

The important thing is to detect the first signs of stress and to act immediately.

The disciplines of personal development allow us to learn methods by which, faced with the first signs of stress, we are able to respond automatically in a different way, entering into, rather than "a state of stress", a state of high performance, with which to effectively face situations.

A common mistake made by those who want to avert stress is to recognize those situations that tend to favor stress responses and to eliminate them.

Do you know what the consequence of this is?

It's a dramatic limitation of choices and opportunities, in addition to the erroneous signal that it is circumstance, rather than us, which determines our state.

We become unable to effectively face these situations, no matter how careful we are to avoid them, when they eventually do occur.

Of course, faced with certain situations which (at the present time) quickly lead us into stress, we might temporarily decide, while we are learning how to choose our psycho-physical-emotional state, to avoid them.

A healthier choice is to take them in small doses, learning to deal with them without accepting stress in our bodies.

"To stress or not to stress" can become a choice.

For more on Averting Stress visit www.guerrillatime.net

61. Managing Stress

The sooner we learn to recognize signs of stress in our bodies, the easier it will be to face them, leading back to a suitable psycho-physical-emotional state.

One choice when you feel stress is to move your body. As you do so, make sure to use your body efficiently, making the minimum effort in your movements.

You can practice being economic by making small, slow movements and noticing in what way you engage your body as a whole, as a system producing those movements, until you discover the most efficient way to make them. Remember to engage your body as a system so as to produce the most efficient (and easiest) movement for you. Unfortunately over the course of our lives we learn inappropriate ways of making use of our bodies. Relearning how to make proper use of our bodies leads to real improvement in our quality of life.

I suggest you explore various methods. Personally I find the Feldenkrais method in its original form, nowadays represented by Mia Segal, a student and partner of Moshé Feldenkrais for many years, to be one of the best for learning how to move more freely, for feeling better and for using the mind and body (careful, it's a metaphor!) in rediscovered harmony.

62. Relaxation

Relaxation is very important for relieving tension, for recouping strength and for putting a spring in our step as we set off upon our various journeys.

Numerous relaxation techniques exist, one of which you have already come across in Guerrilla Time.

Guerrillas of time explore various ways of relaxing and practice until they able to choose those which effectively help them relax.

For more on Relaxation visit www.andreafrausin.com and www.guerrillatimebook.com

63. Performance

Our performance, our behaviors, strongly depend upon the psycho-physical-emotional state in which we find ourselves.

As you've heard me repeat many times, learn to choose your state and the quality of your performance and your life will increase considerably.

Guerrillas of time learn how to automatically enter into high performance states that allow them to live a life of extraordinary quality while also helping them to achieve previously unimagined results.

NLP New Code, nurtured from its beginnings as NLP through to its improved present evolution as NLP New Code thanks mainly to the work of Dr. John Grinder, offers extraordinary tools for choosing your state, enhancing performance and increasing the quality of your life and well-being, tools which draw upon the potential of the unconscious mind.

For more information, visit www.andreafrausin.com

64. Physical Order

Plan your personal order in a way which is for you effective: effective, for example, when you need to find something fast; effective, for example, in allowing you to live in a clean and healthy environment.

If you are working in a team, consider the other members of the team. You can't be sure that order for you is order for them.

When you have only yourself to think about, choose an order that works best for you.

Learn new methods and test them until they become a possible choice. We can always learn how to make ourselves better.

65. The Power of Breaks

Nowadays we tend to forget about the almost magic power of breaks, which allow us to regenerate and to increase our satisfaction and productivity.

Many people have learned that, when feeling a little down on energy, rather than taking 3 or four minutes to recoup their energies (something our bodies do naturally) and setting off again with renewed vigor, a coffee is the best solution. A cup of coffee can be a great idea, when it doesn't become an addiction, when it's not the only way to stay awake in the morning or the only way to get through the morning.

Find alternatives. For example, having a walk outside in the fresh air for a few minutes can be quite reinvigorating.

Or just having a break, observing something you like and breathing in the most appropriate way for you.

Regular short breaks (rely on how you feel to know how regular) allow you to easily restore your energies, respecting the natural rhythms of your body.

You will notice that you are more productive and have a higher quality of life.

66. Earnings

What's the profitability of your time?

If considering your time in business terms, this is a very important question.

How many people, entrepreneurs, managers, consultants, employees find themselves doing extremely low added-value activities just because… they are used to doing them?

These are activities that normally have little to do with one's role and give little added-value from the point of view of the person who does them.

What profits do you get from your work time?

Surely, as you well know, this is not the only question for a Guerrilla of time.

Guerrillas of time, even when it comes to business, take account of the satisfaction they get from what they do. They know that with satisfaction the quality of their work increases along with profitability.

67. Method

The only effective method is the one that works for you!

Bear it in mind always.

Many suggest methods which they say work.

Guerrillas of time put them all to the test, practice them until they become options and only keep what works… for themselves.

This is the human factor. It's you that makes the difference.

68. Keep It Simple

One of the main things to remember when reading *Guerrilla Time*, in its application and also very often in life is: Keep it simple.

You have a ton of ideas and suggestions in this text. Use them as brainstorming inputs, sleep on them, practice, practice, practice and then: Keep it simple.

69. Plan for the Unexpected

Do you tend to plan every single moment of your day?

Research has demonstrated that unforeseen happenings can easily account for (and can even exceed) 50% of our work time.

If you plan everything and, for example, 30% of your time goes into dealing with unforeseen events, then 30% of the things you had planned to do won't get done and… you'll feel ineffective, you'll start to doubt the importance of planning or, even worse, you'll start to doubt yourself.

What to do then?

First of all, measure the amount of time which normally gets taken up in unforeseen circumstances. Even though this quantity may vary, you'll discover you can do something extremely clever.

As you plan, plan time for unforeseen occurrences, a little more than the average time you notice these things taking up.

If unexpected things don't happen, no problem: Having also made a plan for the week, on the day everything does go to plan, you can dedicate yourself to other priorities and things to be done that week, getting ahead in work and having in any case time for any other unexpected events that pop up.

You'll discover that planning is a great tool at your disposal, if used correctly.

70. One Thing at a Time

Various studies confirm the importance of focus, of concentrating our attention on one thing at a time, especially if that thing is important, strategic or is a priority.

We are pushed towards multi-tasking, into doing many things at once.

Stop for a second and ask yourself: "What's my intention?"

If your intention is to be effective and efficient, then do one thing at a time.

You're not convinced? You seem to do more things better and quicker when multi-tasking?

Put what I'm saying to the test.

If you're at your computer doing something important, close other programs, alerts and any other superfluous paraphernalia that might distract you and focus on what you are doing.

After a while, you'll find you're doing better, working faster, and you'll probably finish the day with greater satisfaction and energy.

71. The "Gandhi Principle"

"It is far easier to do what one knows how to do than it is to do what is needed."

I have repeatedly spoken about habits, about their advantages and their disadvantages.

In situations undergoing rapid change, in which the scene is prone to abrupt and drastic mutation, what we know how to do (in that we've had some practice at it) may not always be the best thing *to do*.

Our goal should be to learn how to constantly learn and one fundamental piece of learning is how to conduct a relationship with that most important of individuals: the self.

This is the core of Guerrilla Time.

It is also important to constantly check if we are doing what we are doing in the most efficient and effective way in terms of our intention.

If this isn't the case, change is the road we must walk.

Remember that when we learn new things, tread new paths, explore new territory, we may experience peculiar sensations; feelings of confusion or annoyance may be no more than indicators that what we are about to do is new. That's why I invite you to practice, practice and practice. To make new things familiar, make them yours, really yours, at your disposal, new options ready to use.

Guerrillas of time know that one of the most significant challenges is to know oneself.

On the temple of the Oracle in Delphi we read: "Nosce te ipsum" (know yourself).

Never has a more sensible imperative been given.

72. Parkinson's Law

"Work expands so as to fill the time available for its completion."

As such, the time you intend to assign to an activity is strategic.

How much time do you think you'll need?

An hour? Of course, and maybe only one.

Half an hour? Absolutely, and perhaps not a minute more.

Learn to test yourself.

For instance, plan to spend a little less time on activities you are familiar with and see what happens.

You might be surprised to find out how Parkinson's law works.

Do your appointments last an hour? For next week, plan to do 5 of them in half the usual time and check if the quality of your results is similar to that achieved in your hour long appointments; it might even be higher.

Of course there are limits to this process and the whole thing must be carried out in consideration of your psycho-physical-emotional state.

Test what I've told you as if it were a game and you will find that you have more time for the things that really count.

73. The Power of Silence

In a society of noise, silence has a magic power.

When we leave a noisy city, or those places in which jarring and intrusive sounds dominate, we are left under no illusions as to when we have indeed left. We quite consciously notice the difference, let's say, as we move into the countryside or the mountains, surrounded by the sounds of nature. In such places we rediscover silence and its discreet and magic power.

As we re-enter the cacophony, to begin with the sounds are sharper and louder; we become aware of the bombardment of noise to which we are subjugated. Then we get used to it. The noise seems to fade away to background chatter. And yet various studies have shown that it has effects on us anyway, whether we notice it or not.

When carrying out any of your daily activities, or simply when wanting to pass the time, notice the sounds around you and ask yourself if you there's something you can do to reconquer, at least in certain moments, the silence.

New energies will free themselves inside you and many surprises await you.

74. Inner Silence

Not only is our external world rich in sounds, noises and chatter... our internal world is too.

Stop for a moment and listen to yourself. Does your internal voice speak? For example, right now, as you are reading, precisely how are you reading? It's likely that you are subverbalizing, meaning you are using your internal voice to read words you learned to read aloud long ago. When looking at things, when walking, when doing any task:

Do you hear an internal commentator commenting on your external experience? This comment, this voice (or voices at times) is called your internal dialogue.

You must have noticed that when you're on top of your game in any given activity, this dialogue is no-where to be heard; there's internal silence and all senses are focused towards the external in the here and now, interacting with the immediate environment to reach the goals you've set yourself.

You must have also noticed that your internal dialogue is present at times when you could easily do without it. For example, you meet someone for the first time and you miss his/her name when told it, precisely because... you were talking to yourself inside.

At times internal dialogue can even be enjoyable, it can keep us company, in the shower perhaps.

The point is: Do you have the choice to remain silent internally?

The quality of your performance and the quality of your life will often depend upon this choice.

75. Alone — With Others

How much time do you spend on your own?

How much with other people?

Are these choices? Or would you prefer that these quantities of time were different?

What's the quality of your time when you are on your own?

How do you spend time with other people? How much of it is in person, how much on the phone or via video conferencing, how much via chat rooms and the like?

What's the quality of your time with other people?

What would you like to improve?

How?

76. Delegate

Learning how to delegate effectively is a must for Guerrillas of time who hold positions of responsibility.

Delegating means giving authority to another person so that he/she has the power and the instruction to reach objectives and fulfill tasks.

Overall responsibility still lies with the delegator, while the delegate is responsible for the delegated tasks.

There may be various obstacles to a delegation, perhaps on behalf of those who give it, perhaps on behalf of those who receive it, perhaps residing in the context in which the delegation finds itself given.

Those who should delegate often don't know how to. They may feel they are giving away power and so they avoid delegating (thus finding themselves performing activities of low added value, without the chance to dedicate their time to activities which are more stimulating and productive for themselves and for the organization). They may have had negative experiences of delegation and for this reason have decided "delegating is not good…".

The consequences are various and can be toxic. For instance, there are businessmen, entrepreneurs and managers who, by avoiding delegation, have sacrificed their lives solely and exclusively to the altar of work, without this having been a deliberate choice.

Obstacles may arise on the side of delegates. Perhaps they lack the essential knowledge or skills needed to effectively carry out their delegated tasks. Perhaps they are afraid to take on extra responsibility. Perhaps…

When faced with the issue of delegation, Guerrillas of time consider all possible obstacles and create a context best suited to the delegation, drawing from it maximum benefit for themselves, for others and for the organization.

Delegation has various advantages:

- it gives value to one's own time and to that of others;
- it allows people to grow by learning to do different things with their knowledge and skills;
- it creates the context for mentors, who transfer part of their expertise and skills in order that their co-workers grow and develop;
- it creates an organizational climate which supports growth and personal development as well as personal responsibility;
- it increases personal and organizational efficiency and effectiveness;
- it increases personal and group satisfaction with a strong impact on people's quality of life.

Key variables for a delegation can be summarized as:

- defining the who: choosing the right person as delegate is fundamental. Making sure this person has (or is developing) the necessary knowledge and skills for the tasks entailed by the delegation is crucial;
- defining the what: many times the delegator is not precise; what is being delegated must be carefully defined, as well as what is specifically expected from the delegate, defining SMART (Specific Measurable Achievable Realistic Time) objectives and making sure the delegate understands correctly;
- defining the how: if the delegate has the necessary knowledge and skills, the delegator simply defines the what, leaving the "how" to the delegate; this isn't possible with beginners to the specific context of a particular delegation; beginners must first be helped to grow, initially being given very precise instructions on the "how" and then gradually receiving less and less input from the delegator as they gain the key knowledge and skills inherent to the specific delegation;
- defining the monitoring: the delegator should always make sure to have a way of monitoring what is being delegated; a monitoring plan must be defined (with scheduled checks); then, to the delegate, it must be made clear what is needed by the delegator for the monitoring of the delegation process.

There are various methods and tools for effective delegation.

Guerrillas of time learn these methods and test them, augmenting their delegation skills, never forgetting that, when they delegate, the human factor is an essential part of the process.

77. Managing Conflict Situations

How do you react in situations of conflict?

Do you have a particular preference?

For example, do you find yourself running away? When you're faced with conflict do you find a way not to face it?

Or do you find yourself trying to win at all costs, even by humiliating the person you're speaking to?

Or do you freeze up, immobile, at the mercy of events, unsure of what to do?

Or…something else?

Understanding your preferences helps you plan a development program… for your preferences.

Having more choices at hand, such as being able to weigh up your motives, balancing them with those of the other people in play, allows you to find new ways to make your life (and not only yours) better.

Conflict situations seem to be on the increase these days. Knowing how to manage them would be wise even if we thought them rare.

78. Negotiating

Being able to negotiate is a very important skill for Guerrillas of time. Negotiation opens up new areas and new opportunities, allowing us to get the best from situations, even those of conflict.

Knowing how to negotiate time, not only with others but also with yourself, helps you find your own personal balance, even in challenging situations, leading to healthy and fruitful personal relationships.

79. Time for Yourself

Many people declare that they really do not have time for themselves. These people often live lives light years distant from the ones they desire to live.

What about you?

How much time do you dedicate to yourself?

How much time is truly for you?

When you take time for yourself, you are not actually taking it away from other things or other people. You are investing your time in the most effective way (and the most productive, if you're interested in productivity) and this will allow you to give much greater value to the time you dedicate to everything else.

80. Passion

Passion cannot be bought at the local store. It's born from within. And as you practice this book's tools, ideas and methods you will discover new passion flowing from inside of you.

You are the real star of this book. As you learn how to better know yourself, you'll discover how to make your passion emerge.

And you'll encourage others to do it too.

81. Talents

People ask themselves: What's my talent? Or worse: Do I have *any* talent?

The questions we ask ourselves have a strong impact on us.

For example, the question "Do I have talent?" leads us to consider that we might not have any talent at all. If we pose the question at the wrong moment (i.e. when our psycho-physical-emotional state is not adequate) we might answer negatively, thus making a grave error and running the risk of influencing our entire lives, believing ourselves to have no talent at all. And we know the impact that self-fulfilling prophecies can have.

Asking ourselves "What's my talent?" leads us to look for a talent.

The truth is that each of us, every one, has many talents. You have many talents!

They are talents that are simply waiting to emerge.

And for them to emerge, it's necessary that you are able to choose your state and that you're able to enter high performance states in the situation you want them to emerge in.

States function as powerful master-keys. They open numerous doors, giving us access to our talents, to as yet unrealized potential, finally letting us see our talents in action, driven by a clear intention.

And do you know what else?

You can augment your talents by cultivating the key skill of a Guerrilla of time: learning to learn. Learning is the chance for us to acquire knowledge from those who have particular skills in specific sectors; sectors in which we desire to excel, skills that in some cases took a long time and many fortuitous events to develop. And the extraordinary thing is that, if we learn to learn, we don't need to dedicate our entire life to developing these special talents. Instead we need only observe these especially capable people at work in their fields of expertise, activating our learning capacities as we do.

New doors open. New universes for exploration become available to the intrepid learner.

A discipline was born with this intention: Neuro-Linguistic Programming. I invite you to explore it with curiosity and in particular the original method that was the foundation of the discipline: the so-called "NLP modeling" (learning through unconscious absorption).

Guerrillas of time learn how to make their talents emerge. They learn how to develop talents and to put them into action for a life of enormous quality.

82. Commitment and Determination

Some of the greatest discoveries, inventions and events occurred thanks to the commitment and determination of certain people; people like you, who, committing themselves with great determination, committing all their energy to their quest, were successful in accomplishing things that others—perhaps with more opportunities, more resources or even more "genius"—came nowhere near to accomplishing.

The commitment and determination being asked of you in this book is to practice, to practice and to practice again with the tools proposed on its pages. Simply knowing what's written here pales in comparison to the new choices and new opportunities that will open before you once you are acting with commitment and determination.

And then… once you've made these methods, ideas and tools your own, they will be part of you, becoming choices truly available to you for when you need them.

83. Constant Learning

One of the keys to living a life of elevated quality and satisfaction is constant learning.

Guerrillas of time know this. They enjoy the learning process as much as they enjoy the new and extraordinary achievements which the learning process inaugurates.

84. Learning from Others

In this text, I insist a great deal upon the "know thyself" approach, upon learning things from ourselves which make our lives better.

This is fundamental.

Other people, too, can be an endless source of learning and satisfaction. We are social animals. We live in relation to others and we can learn a world of things from those around us (not to mention nowadays from those far from us as well).

Guerrillas of time constantly learn from themselves and they constantly learn from other people so as to make their own lives better.

85. Personal Development

Constantly learning, both from ourselves and from others, is part of a process that a Guerrilla of time understands and practices. This process is known as personal development.

New opportunities to bring out the best in ourselves come from progress made by the methods and techniques of personal development.

Guerrillas of time know this, and are very attentive and curious with regard to such discoveries, willing to apply everything that has the power to improve their lives.

For more on Personal Development visit www.andreafrausin.com

86. Change

People say change is the only constant in the human condition. And yet we human beings are often resistant to it. We carry on behaving in ways that prove unsuitable with regard to our intentions. Habits.

Learning how to change our habits—how to benefit from opportunities without repeating the same unsuitable patterns and behaviors—is extremely important.

It's not only a matter of efficiency and effectiveness in terms of our objectives:

Learning to change and being able to choose how to change allows us to get the best out of life.

87. Here and Now

In our hypermodern, technological, frenetic society, adults seem to have lost a ability children often practice with curiosity and amusement: the ability to live the moment, to live the here and now.

How many times a day do we find ourselves in front of someone who is speaking to us while we're thinking of what we're going to do next; or of something that happened a while ago; or... of anything else which is not the sensorially rich experience of the present moment?

How often do we realize, embarrassingly late, that the person next to us is talking... *to us*?

How often do we jump at the touch of someone we know well, someone who comes up to us slow and steady from the front, under the illusion that we see him or her?

In each of these moments, we're not present... in the present!

Not living in the here and now can be a natural choice. We can shift from one psycho-physical-emotional state to another. In one we think, internally producing images, sounds and feelings, separately or combined. In another we relax. In other we plan the future, creating things inside ourselves that haven't yet happened and that we presume will happen. In another we look back at past things and relive them...

But what happens if we no longer have the choice to live in the here and now, in the present moment? What happens if, on autopilot, we are constantly flit between past and future, losing sight of the present, the only thing real thing we have?

Imagine you're with a dear friend and you really want to dedicate your time and attention to him or her, but you are continuously distracted by a coming and going between past and future. You're with the person you love and you don't realize she has changed her hair color. You're walking, unaware of the sensations emanating from your body, warning you of a change in the terrain and… you crash sprawling to the ground .

Like this we are victims… unable to enjoy the most precious gift we have—the moment we are living right now!

Take small moments of the day just for yourself, 10 minutes should be enough. Yes, just for you. Act as you wish, do what you feel like doing in the moment, without any planning. Breath slowly and focus your attention upon the present sensory experience. See what you see, listen to the sounds around you and feel your body as it moves.

Do it regularly, day after day, and slowly you'll reopen doors, you'll rediscover choices that give every single moment a special meaning; every single second becomes unique and special.

Enjoy your exploration.

88. Past

Many people remain trapped in the past. They speak about it constantly, they relive it constantly.

With what intention?

If the intention is to learn from experience so as to live a better life, here's some news:

If we relive the past, the only thing we'll learn is to repeat the behaviors that we'd prefer to be rid of.

The good news is that the past is history, done, finished.

And the disciplines of personal development teach us how to learn from errors without falling into the swamps of the past and how to fully live the present whilst planning the future.

89. Future

There are many people who live in the future. They keep on talking about tomorrow, or the day after tomorrow and, at the same time, scarcely live in the present. Being able to think of the future, as being able to think of the past, without being negatively influenced by it, is a great ability.

Careful: Being able to live the only thing we truly have is a crucial skill for a Guerrilla of time. Live the here and now.

90. Real Free Time

Do you give yourself time that is really free?

Many people have learned to plan their lives so meticulously that, meticulously, they plan their time which is…*free*.

Learn to leave yourself gaps, perhaps small gaps, in which your time is really free.

Plan 15 minutes of your day for doing whatever you feel like doing in those fifteen minutes. No plans allowed for those 15 minutes. Make a habit of it, enjoy discovering what you really want to do in those 15 minutes… and do it!

91. Choosing Your State

One of the key skills of a Guerrilla of time is the ability to choose his/her own psycho-physical-emotional state.

92. Life Dynamic Balance

We live in a complex world, full of hazards and opportunities.

Guerrillas of time learn to dynamically balance their lives so as to live the gift of time as one of the biggest opportunities they have.

93. Food

The quality of the food we eat has a profound impact on how we feel, on our health and on the quality of our lives.

The following advice should in no way take the place of the advice given by doctors and nutritional specialists, and yet it may be of use to any who are "fighting" with their weight or who simply would like to have a new food experience.

First of all, change perspective: It's not about fighting your weight or controlling it. Think, instead, about forging an alliance with yourself such that your body takes on a more appropriate shape (that is, aligned with your physical structure and needs, and not with images imposed by society). It is essential to overcome the logic of opposition and hostility toward ourselves: "partnership" with ourselves can actually produce results we wouldn't have dreamed of.

Another essential step is to remaster the sensations emanating from our bodies. In our society, many of us, much of the time, live our lives as if we were separate from our bodies (out of body experiences not included). There are various remedies for this "bad habit". For instance, we can find the time to sense our bodies at intervals, fully paying attention both to tactile sensations externally and to visceral sensations internally. An interesting experience may be to take three steps (three normal steps) over the course of twelve minutes or so, rather than the usual one of two seconds it would take, paying attention to sensations. You can then repeat the practice with other "common" actions. Having the choice to sense your own body is very important in the context of food (and not only then). This is especially important when we start to feel hungry rather than when we are already starving. When we start to feel hungry, it is time to eat.

It's time to eat what specifically? Well…whatever we physically perceive to be an effective response to our hunger. Then we assess the consequences after having eaten—do we feel bright and breezy or bloated and bogged down?

How should we eat specifically?

How many of us are used to eating sat in front of the computer, or while watching TV, or while interacting with other people? How many eat in 5 minutes or less?

When we eat, it's important that we do it savoring every single mouthful, tasting it to the full. At the beginning, to re-educate ourselves, it may be useful to put down fork, spoon or sandwich between mouthfuls so as to enjoy the full satisfaction of eating.

We'll rediscover tastes. We'll discover that some of the things we were eating are not exactly those things which we need to eat. We'll eat what we need to eat and not much, much more. All because we'll be paying more attention to the sensations from our bodies.

Until when should we eat exactly?

Until we are satisfied, and not until the moment we are about to explode.

When we feel satisfied, it's time to stop, even if we haven't finished our plate and the accusing gazes of fellow diners suggest we should eat it all ("... think of the poor children in Africa...")

None of this is easy. It requires changing entrenched habits and it requires the progressive reacquisition of contact with our bodies and our sensations.

Following these suggestions, you'll notice various pleasant side effects in other parts of your life as well.

94. Air

Very often we forget to do something fundamental to life...we forget to breathe. Notice your breathing in different moments of the day. You'll see that, when you're not feeling good, your breathing tends to freeze up, it's rhythm quite different from when you're feeling good and full of energy.

Remember to breathe. Whenever and wherever.

And remember to take a breath of fresh air every now and then.

95. Water

Something as simple as drinking water when we're thirsty makes a big difference to how we feel and has a profound impact on our behaviors and our choices. Be sensitive to your body and its water needs and drink water when feel you need to.

Carrying a bottle of water with you may help you to remember to drink when you feel thirsty.

96. Movement

We are designed to move.

Alas, people forget this fact too often.

Consequences include excessive weight, muscle and bone pain, reduced sensitivity to one's own body and its needs and various other health problems.

Move!

You don't need to run obsessively, or to make a daily attempt to surpass the physical limits of man. When the chance for a walk presents itself, walk. Take the stairs and not the elevator. Ride a bike here and there, to the shops, to work, for pleasure. Make simple movements. Avoid excessive effort and… do it on a daily basis.

A Guerrilla knows our experience of life is heavily conditioned by the movement we make and the way in which we make it—we are designed to move after all.

How could you increase your movement and the quality of your movement during your day?

For more on Movement visit www.andreafrausin.com

97. Sleep

Sleeping well allows you to recover your energies, to process your experiences so as to make fruitful use of them and to wake up refreshed, energized and ready for a wonderful new day.

Not only is the quantity of sleep important (on which much research has been conducted), but quality, too, matters enormously.

So how long to sleep for?

There are no correct answers to this question. Some studies propose themselves as the final word on the question. Others equally sure of themselves contradict these first. Don't put your trust in averages, which don't take account of subjectivity, of your personal idiosyncrasies or of sleep quality, an essential factor.

Assess by experience what's for you the best amount of time to sleep. Be sensitive to your body, to how you feel and to your needs.

Guerrillas of time greatly value knowing the right number of hours they need to get a good night's sleep.

98. Information

We live in an information world and we are constantly bombarded by information. But what information is relevant to us? What information gives us that added value we need to improve our lives?

There are people who, in this sea of information, have become lost. They survive by "feeding" on irrelevant information, at times on damaging information.

Others decide to withdraw to the hills, frightened by the sheer bulk of available data.

Guerrillas of time know how important information is and play an active role in selecting the information that will improve the quality of their time and the quality of their lives.

There are several ways to get informed and technology helps us here… if we know how to use it.

99. Searching for Information

We are bombarded by information, though not always by the information that interests us. This mass of rather useless information causes us to lose our way and to lose sight of what we need most in order to improve the quality of our lives.

Which sources of information are you currently using?

Are they the result of choices?

Are they the result of research?

Or are they the result of past habits?

And if they are the result of habits, are they still responding to your needs?

Do they respond to your intentions?

What other sources are you not using?

Talk to the people who you consider to be most informed and ask them which sources of information they use. Actively research information sources which may help you in the pursuit of your objectives.

Today technology allows us to remain constantly informed.

A Guerrilla knows how to make good use of it.

100. Search Engines

In order to search for information on the Internet, the first thing to learn is how to use search engines.

Google, the most used (www.google.com), Yahoo (www.yahoo.com), Bing (www.bing.com).

Have a look at the settings and learn how to customize them so as to get the desired results via your searches.

There are a number of online guides that teach you how to better use search engines.

101. Selecting Information

Selecting information requires focus, it requires speed, it requires that we check various sources so that we can then choose the ones that interest us.

All this may need some time. The Internet has the power to be a blessing or a bain. Then there are non-internet based sources.

102. Feed RSS

Do we want to rapidly access a variety of information that interests us from different web sources, receiving updates, without having to "visit" these sources singularly one after the other?

If so, then it might be useful to understand how to use RSS (Really Simple Syndication) Feeds, which, although they've been around for a while, aren't used by many people to select information and stay informed.

RSS Feeds are normally accessed with the help of an aggregator. The user can automatically receive content from blogs, websites or other RSS enabled sites without directly accessing the site.

How to best use RSS Feeds?

1. Get an aggregator (a feed reader or newsreader). An aggregator is either a site or a desktop program which gathers content from RSS enabled sites and displays it to the user.
2. Choose your favorite RSS Feeds
3. Update your favorite sources and add to them

And you're done!

At this point you only need access your feed reader (on your computer, tablet or smartphone) and receive updates from your favourite sources.

103. Newsletter Subscription

Another way to stay informed is to subscribe to high added value newsletters.

Once again, the rule is to select your sources. Ask yourselves: Do I need the information provided by this newsletter?

If in doubt, give it a try and if it doesn't work, unsubscribe (it's your right.)

The time dedicated to information is time well spent if the information is quality... for you.

104. Alerts

To keep updated about something, be it topic, product, person, business or even yourself (to know who's speaking about you online), you can use Google Alert.

This service sends you emails or feeds about your queries.

Here's what you need to do:

- find *google alerts* via your search engine and access the site;
- enter your gmail account username and password (if you don't have one, you can create an account then and there);
- write your search query, for example Andrea Frausin;
- choose which results you want to be displayed: all / news / blog / video / discussions / books;
- choose the update frequency: occasional / daily / weekly
- choose the quantity: only the best results / all results;
- choose how to display them: email or feed;
- click on "create alert".

From now on, you will receive updates in your mailbox or via your feed aggregator.

Besides Google, there are other alerts, for example Yahoo. Look for others that might be useful to you.

Guerrillas look for solutions that help them improve their lives, simplifying complexity and using technology in a clever way.

105. On-line Calendar and On-line To-Do List

Many web based email services (including Google and Yahoo) also provide an on-line calendar.

It is easy to sync this calendar with the default one on your computer, tablet or smartphone, always having the same updated agenda on all your devices.

You can also directly insert your to-do lists, setting up deadlines and alarms for appointments and things to do.

106. E-mail

Email is a must for a Guerrilla of time.

When getting organized, one of the first questions Guerrillas of time ask themselves is:

Which tools shall I use?

With what intention?

Email can be a very precious tool which can either simplify our lives or... make them worse.

The following is a list of simple rules on how to use email:

1. First of all, ask yourself: What is my intention in wanting to write this email?
2. Then ask yourself: Is email the best tool to satisfy my intention?

Email, for instance, is often badly used in businesses. An issue that would normally take a one minute call may need several emails. Email is only text, therefore it doesn't provide an immediate feedback and has no other elements of communication in it (no paraverbal or nonverbal clues) to correctly contextualize or interpret the message.

It may be badly used in interpersonal relationships as well—how often do misunderstandings occur because of a bad use of this tool?

First of all, always check that it's the best tool to satisfy your intention. Compare with direct speech, a call, a video conference, chat etc… in general, anything that helps you achieve your objective.

If email is not the best tool, change tool.

If it is still the best one to achieve your objective, read the points that follow.

3. Before writing an email, stand in both the receiver's and an external observer's shoes, then get back to yourself and start writing.
4. If needed, use framing.

Telling the receiver your intention right at the beginning of your message allows the reader to better understand the context within which the rest of your message falls.

If, for example, you want to ask the receiver for some information, clearly stating your request is very useful to this person, who will better understand your goal, and to you, who will have more chance of getting what you want.

If, on the other hand, you want to send feedback, stating your intention may help you deliver your message in accordance with your intention.

5. Put yourself once more in the receiver's shoes

Is the email clear? Comprehensible? Does it achieve the goal that the sender (you) had set?

Improve your text, until, from the perspective of the receiver, it seems effective.

6. For important emails, let some time pass and read them again before sending.

There are never-ending tales of emails which have caused breakups, firings, misunderstandings, etc. which then took years to be amended…

When reading it again, put yourself in three different pairs of shoes: you first, then the receiver, then an external observer. Then finish in your shoes: are you satisfied now?

To avoid an early sending of the message in error, write the receiver's address after re-reading it and testing it to your satisfaction. Also remember to save the draft.

7. Emails are written material, they can be shown and used in another context, shown to other people—remember this when you are writing and reading. It is easy to send an email, as it is easy to have very unpleasant consequences with a negative impact on your quality of life.

Other useful suggestions for your emails:

- Periodically check your spam folder. Some email providers automatically activate spam filters. They are very useful, sparing you hours of trashing undesired email. Sometimes, though, they make mistakes. What if that long awaited message ended up in the spam folder?
- If you check your email on more than one device, consider the IMAP service, which automatically synchronizes all devices;
- sort your email into folders and file messages as soon as possible, leaving the inbox relatively empty, especially if you receive a lot of mail;
- regularly backup your email. Email is an extremely important tool for work and social purposes where a lot of information is recorded. Regularly backup your emails… you never know.

107. E-mail Management: E-mail Writing Skills

Learn to improve your email writing. Every communication tool has its rule, its best practice. Too often we use one communication tool as if it were another.

Do you write e-mails as if you were talking on the phone?

There is no paraverbal communication in emails, no tone, pace, speed or pauses to frame the content, to give special meaning to what we are saying...

There's immediate feedback on the phone. You can ask questions and get an immediate answer, listening to the person's tone, breathing, pace, getting feedback which an email doesn't provide.

Do you write emails as if you were talking face to face?

Face to face, you have verbal, paraverbal and nonverbal communication. An old study found that when two strangers talk about something about which only one of them knows something, the communicative impact is distributed along the three "channels" as follows:

- 7% is verbal communication (content)... yes, only 7%.
- 38% is paraverbal (all the attributes of voice tone, pace, volume, speed...).
- 55% is nonverbal communication (posture, gesture, mime).

Email has no paraverbal and nonverbal communication.

In emails you cannot get immediate feedback. For instance, nonverbal responses that normally occur in dialogues.

On the other hand, with just a simple email you can communicate with a potentially endless number of people all over the world.

Every tool has its own characteristics, its pros and cons.

Before using them, ask yourself: Does it satisfy my intention?

108. E-mail Management: Reading

When you read an email, how do you read it?

Such a question may at first sound strange. However, strange it is not.

Guerrillas know how important psycho-physical-emotional states are in "filtering" our experiences.

Before starting to read your email, notice your state. If it is not suitable, change it before reading your email.

Have you already started reading without checking your state?

Stop for a while. This is crucial especially if:

- the email is very important to you;
- the email features criticism of you;
- the email features content which, for you, is moving or sensitive.

Stop and change your state. Then read again.

Once again, the first question: When you read an email, how do you read it?

Do you read as most people do, internally verbalizing words? If so, with which voice are you reading, with which speed, volume, pace? Our communication not only influences other people—it also influences ourselves.

Do you remember the impact of paraverbal communication?

When verbalizing, what kind of paraverbal communication are you using? How is it influencing your interpretation of the email?

If it's an important mail, read it with the sender's voice (if you've ever heard it); with his/her tone, pace, rhythm… How do your feelings change when reading it like that? How does your interpretation change?

According to the way we verbalize, we can give the same message different meanings and interpretations.

And we can't know which interpretation is the right one.

Guerrillas love choices and consider different interpretations of the same message. Thus their responses will be more effective.

109. Gmail, Yahoomail, Outlook and Other Free Email Providers

There are several free tools for email, and they're all of great value. If you haven't done it yet, open a Gmail account and check its functions.

I suggest you check the settings. You can create personal folders, import messages and contacts from other accounts. If you have other email addresses, you can use Gmail to access them and to send emails from those addresses. You can activate IMAP, you can work offline from a standard browser, chat, do videoconferencing, etc…

Open a Yahoo email account and spend some time checking its features. You might discover some free services and take advantage of the competition among providers.

Then choose your favorite email address and use it to retrieve email from other accounts as well, in order to have everything in one place.

110. Google+

Google+ can be used for free to get in touch with other people on the web or to effectively manage a series of contacts.

You can share what you think, share links and pictures with groups, have a video conference with several people at the same time, participate in group chats, upload pictures or videos from your mobile and keep a copy online or share them, and much more.

If some of the above mentioned tools might improve the quality of your life, all it takes is a free Gmail account. Google+ has been online since June 2011.

111. Social Networks

Social networks can be a fantastic tool to give our time value, if properly used. First of all, what are social networks?

Social networks are online "places" (platforms) where people with similar interests can interact using e-mail, chat, audio-video communication and instant messaging. Every social network features different types of services. Users, for example, can share files, blog and join and create discussion groups or forums. People can interact as members of an online community in different ways.

The development of social networks has been so remarkable that they are changing the way people interact online: Facebook, Twitter, LinkedIn, MySpace and, recently, Google+ to name but a few.

A Guerrilla of time knows how to get updated, seizing every opportunity technology offers.

Contemporarily, Guerrillas of time are immune to popular trends—they define their intentions, set their own directions and keep wondering: Which tool can best help me move in my chosen direction?

How much time do I need to invest to master the new tool before I can get the benefits I wanted from it?

Is it worth my time?

A Guerrilla of time wants to improve the quality of his/her life. Sometimes sacrifices can bear great results in terms of satisfaction and well-being. A Guerrilla carefully separates what is useful from what is not.

112. Social Networks Management: Avoiding the Addiction Trap

If you want to use social media (or you're already using them), the first question to ask is: Does it satisfy my intention to improve the quality of my life?

If the answer is yes, then it may be useful to ask yourself:

How much time do I need to give to social media?

And then set a limit.

Too many people get lost in social media... and they are still missing...

Not always is this a choice. Sometimes it becomes an addiction.

Guerrillas of time are sensitive to themselves and to what might lead them into addiction. Avoid whatever is not your deliberate choice. Guerrillas of time often ask themselves:

How is what I am doing helping me to live a better life?

113. Skype and Other Video-Audio Communication Tools

Today there are many extraordinary tools that allow anyone with an Internet connection to call or videocall virtually anyone else in the world for free.

You can do it on your PC, smartphone or tablet (if logged on to the Internet via a wi-fi or mobile connection).

Technology is available. Too many people don't know this yet, or simply don't use it. Habits change slowly even when the world moves fast.

Guerrillas of time use these extraordinary tools, taking the necessary time to understand how they work. They know how to choose the appropriate tool: either email, text or appointment. They know how to minimize their movements by maximizing their use of free video-audio communication tools.

114. Video-audio Conference

Free video-audio communication tools allow people to meet for free. The maximum number of interacting people increases week after week. Today we can see each other easily, even half a world away.

Of course, it's not like meeting someone in real life. It's another opportunity, something that, if used, may help the planet become less polluted.

How many ways could you use video-audio communication to improve your life?

115. Managing Contacts

Managing one's contacts has become extremely difficult for some people, taking a lot of energy and time. Technology improves the opportunities to keep in touch with people, especially those sharing the same interests as you, your relatives and much more. Such opportunities may lead you to have so many contacts that it can become complicated to pay due attention and at the same time experience the same satisfaction interpersonal relationships give.

In such a mess and mass of people, most of whom are mere acquaintances, we may easily forget about a very important friend, maybe in an important moment of his/her life.

Remembering everything about everyone, in an ever expanding context, requires a strategy (a clear intention) and a method.

Technology may help us here too.

Among the simple, effective things to do, it may be a good idea to have an updated (and synchronized) calendar with reminders of your appointments, events, anniversaries—a database which automatically feeds and integrates all the "sources" coming from friends and acquaintances.

To name but a few: a phone book (it can be a physical one, although I suggest an electronic one with regular backup to prevent loss of data), social media (Facebook, LinkedIn, Google+ etc).

Such a database should be accessible and upgradeable in different ways and from different devices—online and offline, from PC, tablet or smartphone. New solutions and opportunities are available every day.

Look up CRMs (Client Relationship Management programs can be easily adapted for managing a wide range of friends and acquaintances) and social CRMs. Compare features. Focus on benefits, online availability, smartphone apps, additional features (like automatic searches inside your network based on social media connections; you may find some of your friends know each other), exportability of data (since new and improved opportunities and software are always available, it's better to be sure your data can be easily exported/imported to/from other applications).

Keep updated on the opportunities technology offers—they can be of real added value, letting you do other things with greater satisfaction while effectively managing your precious network of friends, colleagues and acquaintances.

116. Mailing Lists

Make sure your contact management system allows you to send emails to special contact lists or that its possible to easily export groups of contacts with their relative e-mails so as to be able to send the e-mails with other tools.

You are a Guerrilla of time, you stay informed and you know what a specific group of your friends likes—for example, new information on personal development. Send them (and only them), such information. They will surely appreciate it—thanks to your capacity to target important information, you have given them something important.

You might do it more quickly and effectively using social media, though perhaps not all your contacts will have taken the leap from e-mail to networking sites.

If you consider yourself a spreader of potential, tell your friends and contacts the benefits of using technology in a savvy way, inviting them to join you. Keep the human factor in mind—sometimes changing habits involves a psychological "cost", which may feel higher than its expected benefit. Learn to make benefits clear and tangible and keep on insisting, making it easy for them to take part in these new opportunities.

Create different lists according to the interests of your contacts.

If the information you provide has high added value, think about creating a system that "feeds" new contacts automatically, sending information you want to share.

117. Interpersonal Communication

Improving interpersonal communication is a priority for a Guerrilla of time.

The quality of our interpersonal communication deeply influences the quality of our life.

Guerrillas of time know that there are many weapons to help them achieve ever better communication and that their availability increases with the evolution of personal development and communication. A Guerrilla of time keeps looking for new ones.

I'll discuss a few of the communicative weapons that can increase the quality of your life, focusing on the most important and basic ones.

118. Interpersonal Communication: Communication Distinctions and Impact

Communication can be divided into verbal, paraverbal and nonverbal communication.

Verbal communication is content, words and sequences of words.

Paraverbal communication is tone, volume, pace, rhythm, speed and pauses of voice.

Nonverbal communication is what's left—posture, gestures and mime.

What's the impact they have on interpersonal communication?

Which one do you think has the greatest impact?

This next piece of information may surprise you.

A 1972 study by Professor Albert Mehrabian found that in certain instances of communication between parties verbal communication accounts for 7% of the total, paraverbal communication 38% and nonverbal communication 55%.

Does this change your approach to interpersonal communication?

These figures relate to certain conditions present in the cases studied. Yet paraverbal and nonverbal communication have a strong impact even without such conditions.

Guerrillas of time use this information and constantly learn new ways to improve their verbal, paraverbal and nonverbal communication.

119. Interpersonal Communication: State

Guerrillas of time know that their psycho-physical-emotional state influences their behavior in interpersonal communication too.

Do you want to say something important?

Which state are you in?

Is it a suitable state for getting the best from yourself?

If not, before saying anything, do everything possible to change it.

Your psycho-physical-emotional state influences your verbal communication, but mostly it influences your nonverbal and paraverbal communication.

It also influences the relationship between you and the other person.

Careful: the other person's psycho-physical-emotional state will influence the way your message is received, as well as the communication it solicits and, therefore, the relationship between the two of you (the same thing happens in groups).

Ask yourself:

What is the other person's state?

Is the state suitable for my intention?

If not, do something before you start talking, so that you can change his/her state.

For example: you are about to present to a potential sponsor an important project on which you have worked for a long time. As you approach the meeting room you feel tension, your heart's beating furiously, you're short of breath, you feel dizzy. What to do?

Start paying attention to your body as you walk, to its more or less tense parts, to your breathing, to your gait… start to modify these elements until you start to feel better and to access a most positive state.

You walk in with your great state and find a welcoming and smiling person. The person receives a call, her (or his) face changes, her breathing changes; she seems a different person as she swivels towards you, with darkness etched across her features. What to do?

Avoid talking about the project until she changes her state. You might ask her if she wants a coffee, just whatever you do, wait for the state to change… and do anything you can to help the person enter a productive state.

Then?

It's time to talk about the project!

120. Interpersonal Communication: Rapport

Rapport may be defined as the nonverbal relationship established between two people or more people comprising of a sort of nonverbal dance between the participants. It's an unconscious dance that involves them mirroring each other, talking with the same speed and tone, establishing "harmony". When one of them moves, the other follows within approximately 30 seconds.

It's the nonverbal relationship that naturally establishes itself when communication spontaneously flows.

What if there is no rapport?

There are various strategies to create it.

Since the 1970s Neuro-Linguistic Programming (NLP—for more information visit www.andreafrausin.com) has practically introduced a technique called mirroring. If not spontaneously established, rapport may be induced by mirroring of the other person.

Take the same position, move at the same speed, act below the person's conscious awareness (as a Guerrilla of time, you have good intentions, you are looking for a way to improve communication).

Careful: many people know of this technique and seem ridiculous when they use it. Always remember its objective, which may be achieved in other ways (for example, speaking about something the other person likes) and remember: before using it, this technique must become a part of you. Nothing is less communicative than a clumsy monkey doing crude mime in front of you rather than listening to what you are saying.

Practice with friends. Practice up to the point that the technique becomes a part of you. Then forget about it. Focus only on your intention and on your state. The technique will be used spontaneously if needed.

In 1996, the discovery of mirror neurons cast a new light on these dynamics, at last giving a scientifically based explanation to phenomena which have been plane to see for millennia and which the creators of NLP intuitively seized upon and operatively tested.

When you communicate, if your intention is to facilitate communication, make sure you have rapport with the person you are talking with. If your intention is different, do the opposite.

Bear in mind that rapport increases mutual influence on psycho-physical-emotional states. Always make sure you are in a great state.

Guerrillas of time want to experience rapport dynamics, knowing how deep an impact this has on the quality of their (and other people's) lives.

121. Interpersonal Communication: Intention/Consequences

New Code NLP (for more information visit www.andreafrausin.com) devised a simple and effective model which has found various applications in this text: this model is the intention-consequences model.

If applied to communication, this model can be graphically represented as follows:

Intention

communicative behavior ➔ consequences

Intention Consequences

What is our intention in communicating X, where X stands for what we want to communicate?

Is our communicative behavior effective in satisfying this intention? Will the consequences of such behavior satisfy our intention?

What other communicative behavior might we use to satisfy our intention?

These are all crucial questions in terms of communication.

We may have behaved in a certain way with someone and then realized that the result was different from that expected. Let's then ask in which other ways we might satisfy our intention, changing our behavior as long as consequences are not aligned with intention.

This sounds good on a cognitive level. Let's then introduce the human factor.

What heavily influences our communication?

That's right, our psycho-physical-emotional state.

If we have the necessary skills for the task at hand (and if not, let's go get them!), a clear intention (completely aligned with ourselves) and a good state, this, along with our ability to be observant and flexible, is all it takes to achieve our objectives.

Simple, isn't it? Simple, though not easy.

Effective communicators define their objectives, act accordingly and, guided by feedback, adapt their behavior to effectively reach those objectives ("if what you are doing is not working, do something else") all within the context of maximum collaboration between their voluntary and involuntary processes.

Practice, practice, practice allows Guerrillas of time to make this method their own, to improve their communicative choices and to achieve unexpected and previously unimagined results.

122. Interpersonal Communication: First Impression

Learn the methods and tools in this book, increase and keep increasing the number of your choices and opportunities, making them a part of you... and be yourself.

Be nurtured by feedback, look for it, notice how people are different and what positively impresses them. And keep learning.

And remember: "You don't have a second chance to make a good first impression."

123. Interpersonal Communication: Communicate with What Is Known to the Person You Are Speaking to

When we communicate and we want people to understand (there are contexts where our objective may be different) the rule of thumb is: Communicate with what is known to the person you are speaking to.

The questions are:

What do we mean by "known to the person"?

Communicate how, specifically?

In this context, "known" stands for what the person actually knows: preferences in communication (check also "rapport"), ways of processing information, language, culture, personal interests, job, passions...

If I am communicating with a person who loves soccer, what better way than to use a soccer metaphor? It's like scoring an open goal!

If the two of you have shared a nice experience, it may be a good idea to refer to that; using it as a fulcrum to better communicate important things can be a good choice.

Communicating with what is known to the person in front of you concerns every form of language—verbal, paraverbal and nonverbal. For effective communication, using images, metaphors, sounds and experiences requires two main skills: being able to see and to listen to the person; having the necessary flexibility to adjust our behavior to the feedback we receive with regard to our goal.

Guerrillas of time spend time with different kinds of people and learn from such variety. They learn to constantly improve their flexibility so as to make their communication more effective, refining their communication skills and discovering what is known to the person with whom they are talking.

124. Interpersonal Communication: Use Multi-sensory Communication

Every person has a preferred way of receiving and processing information. Of course, these experiences change with time, can be modified and strictly depend on context and on the state the person is in.

A simple rule to remember is to communicate in a multi-sensory way. Use words that evoke vision (e.g. look, glance, eye, clearly, beautiful); use words which relate to sounds (e.g. hear, listen, noisy, harmony); let your language suggest tactile and bodily sensations (e.g. feel, heat, touching). In certain contexts, it's essential to introduce the senses of taste and of smell.

Spend time with people who do not speak or behave like you, who use words that relate to different senses. Gain rapport, talk like them. This will help you learn new ways of expressing yourself and of directly experiencing reality.

Multi-sensory communication allows you to better involve people and to become a more successful communicator.

Multi-sensory communication increases your choices with regard to how you experience reality and its fruits can be enjoyed well beyond the field of communication, having a profound effect on your quality of life.

125. Interpersonal Communication: Proxemics

The distance between people communicating has a strong impact on the communication itself and is something we do not consciously notice. Understanding how these dynamics work is an essential skill for a Guerrilla of time who wants to communicate effectively.

Do the following and notice what happens: As you communicate with people, deliberately change the distance between you and them. Carefully watch how the other person's state changes and how the relationship flows.

You will discover many things.

I strongly advice you, before reading on, to try this and to make note of your impressions and discoveries.

Here are some of the dynamics you will have noticed:

- changing distance directly influences the other person's state;
- in different spaces, people will react to changes in distance differently. For instance, in an elevator a close distance is more acceptable than when outside;
- depending on the other person's state, he/she reacts differently to changes in distance;
- depending on your state, the other person reacts differently to changes in distance;
- depending on your behavior, the other person reacts differently to changes in distance;
- the distance also influences your state and therefore your behavior too;

… (add to these what you yourself have noticed).

So…how to use this information in a practical way?

First of all, practice keeping a good state, regardless of the distance from the other person. Do you feel uncomfortable when people get too close or actually touch you? If you want to improve your choices, train yourself to keep your state, even when people get close or touch you.

Second, keep developing your observation and listening skills. You want to be able to identify the signs (visual or audio) coming from the other person which tell you his/her state or of a change in the same.

Without these skills, we're like blindfolded racing drivers.

Third, learn to change distance according to your intention.

If you feel there's something wrong with the distance between you and the other person, change it and see what happens—see if his/her state improves.

If you step back as the other person gets closer, learn to keep your state.

For that person a much shorter distance may be essential to communicate effectively with you. Your flexibility improves your communication skills.

With better communication the quality of your time dramatically changes and, since communication is effective, you also have more time.

126. Interpersonal Communication: Listening

Being able to truly listen when we want, for how long we want is a great choice available to us. One of the things missing most from our society is the ability to listen.

Attention is hijacked at the speed of light and as a consequence many people experience great difficulty when trying to stay focused and to listen.

Guerrillas of time know how to keep their ears wide open, paying attention to people as they speak.

Guerrillas of time know how to silence their own internal dialogue when it's time to really listen.

Guerrillas of time know the benefits of listening, both for themselves and for others.

127. Interpersonal Communication: Active Listening

Active listening is a tool we should remember and keep to hand. Listening doesn't only mean keeping our ears open, but also actively interacting when needed or appropriate.

Asking questions and interacting on a nonverbal level (see rapport) are just two ways to actively listen.

How many other ways to actively listen do you know of?

128. Interpersonal Communication:
Putting Yourself in Someone Else's Shoes

Always remember to take off your own shoes first!

A famous quote from the field of communication goes:

"The map is not the territory."

Our way of experiencing reality is not reality itself, but rather a representation of it.

Is this representation useful with regard to your intention?

Too often we become trapped in narrow cages... cages we build for ourselves, shaped by our own way of thinking, of seeing reality, of thinking *about* reality.

Guerrillas of time know that reality is subjective. They know that what they think is only a map, and that a map is useful only if it helps us reach our final destination.

Being able to change our perceptual position, standing in the shoes of those who we speak to, is very useful in communication, and not only there. Mirroring is not only a strategy to make communication flow better, but also a way to enter another person's world, experiencing it from within, watching and listening to things in a different way, from that person's point of view.

How do others see us? How do they hear our voices? How do they experience their own bodies? What do they think of us? What are their intentions?

These are useful questions that can help you put yourself in another person's shoes.

Remember, to get into someone else's shoes, you first have to take yours off!

Wearing someone else's shoes means experiencing their position. It's therefore important that you temporarily put aside your own beliefs, convictions, values...

When we come back to experiencing reality in our way, it will be enriched by the differences we experienced when in the other person's shoes.

We will understand more, communicate in a better way and learn useful things to improve our lives.

129. Interpersonal Communication: Taking an External Observer's Perspective

Putting ourselves in other people's shoes is not the only thing we should consider as we communicate. It's also useful and extremely interesting to take the position of an external observer, of someone who looks at a situation from the outside.

With a change in perceptual position, the way we look at the dynamics of a situation also changes, leaving room for new solutions and for more effective relationships and communication.

Guerrillas of time love to change their own perceptual position before making up their mind. Changing position is also a good way to enrich one's point of view.

130. Interpersonal Communication: Using NOT Effectively

Don't think of a blue hen.

And there it is, a blue hen popping into your mind.

Don't think of green.

And there's the green.

Our brain processes given information differently from how we speak that information.

And it processes first that which we deny.

This has many consequences!

How often have you been told NOT to worry, when you were relaxed and not worrying until that moment?

Has it happened to you, when you've been looking at a product you'd have liked to buy, that some clueless shop assistant comes up and says

"Look, this product is a bargain, it doesn't cost much at all" and you naturally wonder, "How much *does* it cost?"

Often in life, we use negative statements that have side effects, leading those to whom we are speaking to think the opposite of what we actually want them to think.

"DON'T run", "DON'T drink", "DON'T smoke…"

These are all good statements, with good intentions—but with what consequences?

Thank God for the Drive *carefully* sign! Without it, why, we'd immediately loose control.

Do you desire more choices and more effective communication for yourself. If so, for the next three months, once a month have a not free weekend and use only affirmative statements.

You will be able to communicate more effectively with regard to your intentions and to influence people around you using negative statements correctly.

It is NOT easy, especially at the beginning. But it will allow you to explore new worlds and to increase your communicative skills and your quality of life.

131. Interpersonal Communication: Say NO Effectively

Many people aren't able to say an, at times, extremely necessary word: NO.

They're at the office, working on something important, needing to stay focused, when a colleague steps into the room and invites them to talk about meaningless things and… they get dragged into a useless discussion.

Or they're mighty tired, can't wait to have a rest, and somebody asks them to do something and… they do it!

It's great to help people satisfy their needs and to contribute to well-being.

It's also essential to think about our own needs.

So, how long do you want to wait before learning how to say no?

Of course, a kind no, so that no-one is offended and you maintain good relations with people.

Do you know people who, even when they say no, make you feel unique and you thank them for saying no?

Let's learn from these people.

Guerrillas of time have many ways to say no, maintaining healthy relationships and respect.

Guerrillas of time respect people and know that, in order to do so, first they must respect themselves.

132. Interpersonal Communication Clarity:
Asking Specific Questions

People often take things for granted, thinking they understand what other people mean.

Most of the time they don't.

I had an accident yesterday.

What did you think as you read this sentence?

Whatever you thought is your internal representation of what you've just read.

I had an accident: I dropped some tea on my pants.

Was it as you thought?

Most likely not.

Questions can be very important when something is not clear to us.

You could have said:

"Accident…?"

…waiting for me to clarify.

"What kind of accident?"

"What do you mean by accident?"

It can also be useful to clarify your intention before asking, so that whoever is listening doesn't end up interpreting your questions as intrusive or some sort of an interrogation; instead they are seen as a way to better understanding.

How many times do we take what others say for granted, giving in to our own interpretations?

How many times does it lead in unexpected directions?

An old saying goes: *Those asking take the lead.*

In this case, we should say: Those who ask questions understand better.

Questions are only one way to specify a person's language.

How many other choices do you have in this regard?

133. Interpersonal Communication:
Use of Informal Communication

Many problems are solved with informal communication. At bars, drinking coffee, at restaurants, eating lunch.

In such moments, a well structured phrase at the right moment can make conflicts disappear like magic. Challenging situations fade away, new opportunities unfold.

134. Telephone Communication

In the age of communication and socialization being able to communicate through different media is very important for our quality of life.

Every medium has its own peculiarities. It's essential to understand them and then to ask ourselves which medium best fits our intention.

The telephone is an extraordinary tool, one which the readers of this book have always had available to them. The universality of mobile phone nowadays makes telephone communication a basic feature for a Guerrilla of time.

135. Telephone vs. Meeting in Person

Consider if the telephone is the best way to communicate what you have to say. Bear in mind that you'll get feedback only via the person's voice. Consider if meeting in person might be more effective.

136. Telephone vs. Video-Audio Communication

Technology allows us to conduct video-audio communication even as we move.

Having the chance to see the person we're speaking to—although different from seeing him/her in person—may be very important for certain types of communication.

How to video-audio call?

There are many free services (Skype, Google Hangouts…) for those using the same software (Skype on Skype, Google Hangouts on Google Talk). Many video-audio systems will soon be integrated into email and social networks.

Do you have a flat rate on your mobile phone? Does your mobile have a camera? Install an app, for example Skype, and you'll be able to video-audio communicate with other Skype users.

It will be ever more possible to access these types of communication. The question to ask, as usual, is: What's my intention?

Which type of communication is most effective, given your intention?

Not having video available may at times be strategic (for example, when you've just got out of bed).

137. Telephone vs. Email ... vs. Combination

Sometimes, such as when you need to keep track of what it is said or written, email can be an alternative or support to a call.

Are you discussing business related topics better kept in written form? Send an email as a report of what's been said and ask the other person for confirmation that what you've written is a good account of what's been discussed.

Or you could send an email and then discuss it on the phone, checking if your intention was satisfied and then send a confirmation email of the resulting agreement.

Using tools correctly and combining them is an essential skill for a Guerrilla of time.

138. Telephone Communication: State

Before calling, check your state: Your state heavily influences your behavior, including the tone of your voice and what you say.

Your voice, on the phone, has a big impact on the outcome of your communication.

Some say nonverbal communication has no influence while on the phone. False!

Nonverbal communication influences your state, which influences your paraverbal communication, which has a big impact on your telephone communication.

Try it out. Call while lying in bed and notice your feedback. Even if the other person cannot see you, he or she can tell from your tone of voice (in a more or less conscious manner) that something is different compared to when you speak while seated or standing. The point is that they will interpret such a difference in their own way, and such interpretation has consequences.

What is your normal position when you call? Do you stay put or move around? How fast do you move?

Have you considered the effect all this has on the effectiveness of your message?

139. Telephone Manners (Etiquette)

Many people, as they call, forget something essential.

We are used to taking our phone with us all the time, even when it is not appropriate. You are in the bathroom and the telephone rings—do you answer? You get out of the shower, the phone rings—same question? You are desperately trying to park your car in a narrow space, pedestrians moving to and fro very close to you—do you answer?

You are in the middle of a traffic jam—do you answer?

Most of the time the answer is yes. This has a big impact on our conversation. And on our quality of life.

Bear also in mind that, as you call, the people may be in one of the above mentioned situations. Bear also in mind that their state heavily influences their behavior.

Is it a strategic call for you? Double-check that the person you are calling is able to pay due attention to you and is in an appropriate state.

Guerrillas of time use tools, they are not slaves to them. Guerrillas of time know psycho-physical-emotional states heavily influence human beings and take this fact into account, in every context.

140. Switch off or Silence That Phone

Watching how people use their phones, it's normal to wonder:

Do you run your phone or is it your phone running you?

It's a basic question if we think in terms of the quality of our lives.

Telephones are extraordinary tools at our disposal. We have *them* at our disposal, rather than their having us at theirs.

We use them so much that often we end up becoming slaves to them, as if we couldn't get by without them. We forget about our intentions. We forget about our objectives.

The tool becomes the master.

Save for a few important exceptions, we can choose not to answer a call.

You are a surgeon, in the operating theater doing surgery, and the phone rings—do you answer? Let's hope you've turned it off and left it outside the room!

Too often we believe we must always answer calls. Is it really so?

If we always answer, and it is not our choice, we allow other people to hijack and reroute our attention.

Every call interrupts what we are currently doing and it is not necessarily easy, afterwards, to start again from where we left off.

If you can manage, not answering every call may be a very clever choice (this does not apply if you are a 911 operator!).

141. Telephone Communication: Privacy

We are traveling on a train and someone at close range is talking on the phone. We can hear every single word, even though what's being said is absolutely confidential. We even hear a credit card number...

Something absolutely to remember when we call in public spaces is that such spaces are... public!

Other people may listen.

Adjust your volume and tone, talk about certain topics knowing that someone may be listening and remember: it's not only a question of privacy.

Guerrillas love to be polite to other human beings, they respect them and are respected.

142. Telephone Communication: When?

Deciding when to call is a very important choice—what state are you in, what state might the other person be in, what's the context, what kind of information do you want to convey, what do you want to communicate?

A very clever choice can be, where possible, to save a certain part of your day for your outbound calls. Your concentration will increase as well as the time for doing other things without being interrupted.

143. Telephone Communication: Use Voicemail

As you begin exploring new choices with regard to managing your telephone (rather than it managing you) you will discover how a tool that's always been there, voicemail, can take on new meaning.

You can record a message to say you are currently busy and unable to answer the call and that you will call back within a certain time.

For urgent matters you can also add a third person to contact and provide a number.

Remember to periodically listen to your voicemail, turning technology into a friend. It may make your life a lot easier.

144. Telephone Communication: Filter Telephone Calls

If you really cannot turn off or silence your telephone when you need to concentrate, you can filter incoming calls. Latest generation smartphones allow you to customize or silence ringtones for specific contacts or groups. If you really cannot refuse a call from your boss or another important person, this can be a really good solution.

145. Telephone Communication: Text

A very simple tool which at hand when you want to communicate with someone is a text message.

Texts are short messages, so it's important to be concise. And remember, as with every written tool there is no real time feedback.

Consider carefully if, given your intention, it's the most suitable tool.

Text messages can be used, as every other weapon of Guerrilla Time, with other tools. If the person you are contacting, for instance, does not read email frequently, you can send a text saying you've just sent an important email.

146. Telephone Communication: Short and Effective Communication

When you call, you're using your precious time and you're asking for the other person's time as well. Remember to ask people if they are able to talk to you at that moment and if they have the time necessary to hear what you have to say. As you listen, pay attention not only to the content of the answer (for example, the word "yes"), but also to the tone. Many people fear causing offence, so they say yes even when they should say no.

If you want your communication to be effective, it's important to learn to listen to people's paraverbal communication, and not solely their verbal communication.

In any case, learning to be concise (and at the same time being able to spend more time on the telephone if needed) is very, very important.

To do that, always ask yourself before calling: What's my intention? Which objectives do I want to achieve with this call? How will I know that I've achieved my objective/s?

Also, remember to put yourself in the other person's shoes before calling, to be back in your own shoes when you make the call and to communicate with what is known to other person.

147. Technology: Smartphone

Choosing the right telephone is very, very important, especially if you have many personal contacts.

Android Phone, iPhone, Windows Phone… all these alternatives need to be carefully assessed.

First of all, be clear on how you will use the phone:

Will you use it to make calls, to send and receive emails, to browse the Internet, to manage your network, to read e-books, etc…?

A smartphone can be used in many different ways—which one would you use the most? Which ones are priority?

Some things to take into consideration before making the final choice:

- screen dimensions and resolution, especially if you frequently use your smartphone to read, send and receive emails or to browse the Internet… your eyes are of great value…
- app availability. Applications can make your life a lot easier in many ways (depending on the operating system running on the phone, you can access various online markets where you can download free or priced apps; some apps are available for more than one platform)
- system speed, for quicker and more comfortable use

- operating system upgrade (will your phone be upgraded in the near future?), to allow your telephone to keep pace with technology
- battery life (any spare batteries or tools to improve its duration, like some phone cases that prolong battery life); this is something to consider, especially if your use your telephone for long periods of time (currently, with intense use, some batteries may not last for an entire day) with no way of charging it (plug, car chargers, etc).

If you want to make video calls with your smartphone, make sure it has a (good) front-facing camera.

Before making up your mind, look for alternatives, ask an expert, consider the pros and cons of every possible choice and, once you've chosen the telephone which best suits your needs, make sure you can find it online, perhaps at a lower price.

148. Technology: Computers

Guerrillas of time choose their computers according to their needs and constantly seek out technology that can help make their lives easier.

Be it a laptop, a desktop or both, the starting point is always the same—how will I use my computer?

If you are not an expert, before asking for any help, you should know what a computer can do for you after you've learned how to use it.

Not only is hardware important—you have to pay close attention to the operating system, which software it comes with and so on. All of these things can improve the quality of your time.

You can also run more than one operating system on your computer, choosing at startup or using virtual machines.

Remember to focus on your needs. If you travel and want to carry your computer with you, think of size, weight and battery life (and possible alternative charging solutions if you cannot access the mains for long periods of time).

Remember to regularly backup your computer. Make it a habit (or, even better, let the computer do it automatically).

149. Technology: Tablet

According to your needs, you might opt for a tablet. There are several types, suitable for almost every need and taste.

Remember to evaluate which operating system is better for you, if it is upgradeable, how easily you can find software (apps), 3G or 4G connection, screen dimensions and resolution, weight, and whatever else might make the difference.

150. Technology: Time Management Software

There are many free and priced time management programs available for computers, tablets and smartphones.

Three things you should consider first. Simplicity, simplicity, simplicity.

Use whatever might help you satisfy your intentions and achieve your objectives.

Sometimes a detailed list with priorities and deadlines may be enough (or more than enough). You can write it down on a piece of paper (be careful not to lose it) or make a digital version of it (remember to regularly back up your device and to sync them all if you use more than one). Keep a calendar.

Sometimes more detailed solutions are needed.

Always start from your needs, aware that user-unfriendly programs end up not being used. Always rely on simplicity.

151. Order On Your Computer

An organized computer makes life a lot easier: at work (a desktop full of files and folders is a terrible sight!); when looking for information (how often we look for files in vain!); when we have to think of our priorities and objectives...

Sort folders according to your intentions, objectives and action plans.

Use programs to make your life easer and remember to back up your computer daily (or at least once a week). The value of the backup drive is best appreciated when your hard drive dies and you lose all your data...

152. Diary / Agenda / Organizer

Be it a paper or an electronic one, it's a simple tool to keep track of your appointments, meetings, things to do, things to remember...

Electronic organizers, which can be easily backed up or synchronized with other devices, make sure you remember what you've planned to do. They are easily customizable—you can decide when to be reminded and how (desktop reminders, emails …).

153. Writing Skills

Being able to write is very important for a Guerrilla of time.

Emails, text messages, posts, tweets, social media updates, letters, books and/or poems (for those who love to write), reports, comments, etc. For them all, you need to be able to write.

Being able to write will help to:

- maintain friendships
- keep in touch
- inform
- share
- apply for a new job
- find new friends
- be well known
- fix appointments
- show your knowledge
- show your skills

Guerrillas of time nurture their own writing skills, read frequently, make note of their own thoughts and ideas, practice writing to better explain themselves and constantly improve this extraordinary communication tool.

154. Yourself, Others, the World

This book is not only for you. Of course, you are the most important person. Yet for each reader of this book there is another you, another person who is the focus of these words. And if each of you who read this book start to live your lives the way you want, if opportunities start to spread like a positive virus, the impact will be felt upon the quality of life of all, even those who have yet to know the secrets of Guerrilla Time.

Our world is an interconnected and intertwined system. If you, like me, like others, start to live as you want, respecting other people and the whole world, we will start something new, a twist, a new way to live that will allow the world to change for the better.

Every journey starts with the first step.

We've just made ours. Forward!

Chapter 7

GUERRILLA TIME GOOD PRACTICES

Best is what you can use effectively!

There are no better weapons than those that you've just read and that you'll practice, practice, practice and that will work for you.

Guerrilla Time is based on the human factor, which, in the end, is you.

You with your dreams, desires and knowledge. You with your skills, competencies and preferences. You and much, much more than these. You are much more than what you've done so far.

I hope that, after you've read and practiced this book, you'll share your experiences with me, as well as any good practices to make this book even more effective both for yourself and for other people. I'd like to leave the world (a little) better than how I found it.

Contact me—you'll find out how at the end of the book.

Looking forward to hearing from you—enjoy your adventures.

Andrea

PS: Re-read this book from time to time. You'll discover and appreciate new things each time.

NEW BEGINNING CONSTANTLY IMPROVE

For further improvements to the quality of your life, to enhance the many themes present in this book, to explore exercises that allow you to draw the best from all corners of experience, and much more besides, I invite you to visit the book's website at:

www.guerrillatimebook.com

For further information on Andrea Frausin visit

www.andreafrausin.com

Contact me at: info@talentigroup.net

Send me your comments, suggestions, feedback, what works for you, what you discover using the tools in this book and… see you soon

Thank you for your attention.

ACKNOWLEDGEMENTS

First and foremost, I wish to offer a heartfelt thanks to you, the reader of this book, who are giving value to the time, to the energy and to the attention that I have dedicated with great passion to this text.

I wish you all the best and that your innermost dreams come true.

THANK YOU!

There are very many people who, directly or indirectly, have contributed to this book and whom I wish to thank from the heart.

I would like to be able to list them all and express to each of them my enormous gratitude.

Since this would require a separate book, I dedicate to each of them all the thanks that follow, especially those after the dots....

THANK YOU

Thank you, thank you, ...

AUTHORS PROFILE

Jay Conrad Levinson widely-known as the Father of Guerrilla Marketing, has been so successful because he has been thinking outside the box ever since he began his marketing career. He was the first to use the term *Guerrilla Marketing* to describe unconventional marketing tools for organizations to use when they have limited resources. Wikipedia says *Guerrilla Marketing* is the best known marketing brand in history. It was named one of the 100 best business books ever written, with over 28 million copies sold. His guerrilla concepts have influenced marketing so much that his books appear in 62 languages and are required reading in MBA programs worldwide. Jay has worked with giant ad agencies, including Leo Burnett and J. Walter Thompson. He developed marketing campaigns for many well-known brands, including the Marlboro Man, the Pillsbury Doughboy, Tony the Tiger, the Jolly Green Giant, Allstate Insurance's *Good Hands*, United Airlines' *Friendly Skies*, and Sears' Diehard Battery.

The Father of Guerrilla Marketing
Author, "Guerrilla Marketing" series of books
The best known marketing brand in history
Named one of the 100 best business books ever written
Over 21 million sold; now in 63 languages

Andrea Frausin is, as he himself likes to put it, "a curious explorer of the human".

A performance and behavioral specialist, he's involved in coaching, training and consultancy. An author, a blogger and a passionate innovator of the themes of personal, professional and organizational development, with an impressive educational background, he is particularly focused on how to join high performance and productivity with well-being and quality of life. Andrea's activities are appreciated at an international level by companies, organizations and private clients, in English and in Italian.

For more on the author you can visit his website at: www.andreafrausin.com

Improve the quality of your life, your performance and your productivity: www.guerrillatimebook.com

www.ingramcontent.com/pod-product-compliance
Lightning Source LLC
Jackson TN
JSHW080202141224
75386JS00029B/985